Making Minds

Making Minds is a groundbreaking work that offers parents, educationalists and policymakers an insight into the scientific research that reveals how we can make minds. Understanding the physical process of learning, like the decoding of DNA, will change how we see ourselves.

Making Minds is also a timely critique of current education systems from one of the most outspoken educational commentators that:

- challenges basic assumptions about learning – and shows the dangers of accepting conventional wisdom
- shows how segregation, prejudice and politics damage education systems – and what should be done about it
- draws on case studies on university admissions, language for young children and degree courses in schools to show how things can change
- demonstrates how new technologies and new research in neuroscience now explain how learning could, and should, make minds.

Paul Kelley is head teacher at Monkseaton High School, UK, and a well-known commentator on education. He is 'at the forefront of scientific and technological advancement in schools' (*The Times Educational Supplement*). The Open University recognized that 'his achievements are undoubtedly making a difference to British education'. Having been involved in education on both sides of the Atlantic, and in India, he is well suited to offer an informed international perspective on the changes that are revolutionizing our understanding of learning.

Making Minds

What's wrong with education – and what should we do about it?

Paul Kelley

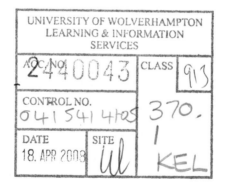

 Routledge
Taylor & Francis Group

LONDON AND NEW YORK

First published 2008
by Routledge
2 Park Square, Milton Park, Abingdon, Oxon OX14 4RN

Simultaneously published in the USA and Canada
by Routledge
270 Madison Ave, New York, NY 10016

Routledge is an imprint of the Taylor & Francis Group, an informa business

© 2008 Paul Kelley

Typeset in Garamond 3 and Gill Sans by
Florence Production Ltd, Stoodleigh, Devon
Printed and bound in Great Britain by
TJ International Ltd, Padstow, Cornwall

Every effort has been made to ensure that the advice and information in
this book is true and accurate at the time of going to press. However,
neither the publisher nor the author can accept any legal responsibility or
liability for any errors or omissions that may be made.

British Library Cataloguing in Publication Data
A catalogue record for this book is available from the British Library

Library of Congress Cataloging in Publication Data
Kelley, Paul.
　　Making minds: what's wrong with education, and what should we do
　　about it?/Paul Kelley.
　　　　　p. cm.
　　　Includes bibliographical references and index.
　　1. Education – Philosophy.　2. Education – Aims and objectives.
　　I. Title.
　　LB14.7.K447 2007
　　370.1–dc22　　　　2006100584

ISBN13: 978–0–415–41410–4 (hbk)
ISBN13: 978–0–415–41411–1 (pbk)
ISBN13: 978–0–203–94680–0 (ebk)

ISBN10: 0–415–41410–5 (hbk)
ISBN10: 0–415–41411–3 (pbk)
ISBN10: 0–203–94680–4 (ebk)

Contents

Introduction

Another change in our world view

From time to time people have had to change their fundamental assumptions about the world. Einstein's theory of relativity transformed the understanding of the universe, and the discovery of DNA revealed the code that determines human development. These revolutions offered new theories, developed from scientific experiments or mathematics, and they led to quite unexpected outcomes – such as black holes and genetic engineering. There is another such revolution under way that will alter our conventional assumptions: discovering how to make minds.

The process of discovery is not being driven by a high-minded quest for understanding everything we think, but rather by simpler issues about understanding the brain and improving learning. In this process of understanding how minds are formed through the growth of the brain and its adaptation to the environment – learning – there is no Einstein, no single genetic code that will explain it all. So this book sets out to describe the journey, and to suggest where we might be heading. The process it describes is extraordinarily all-embracing in some ways, but the underlying principles are, in the end, quite easy to grasp.

This new world view will not come about because people are dissatisfied by new trends in education, or through some revolution driven by new technologies. Our world view will change because we will discover how minds are created, and how to create them. This new understanding will not happen overnight, nor will the outward face of formal education evolve rapidly – at first. Yet in the end the world will, literally, never be – or even appear to be – the same.

The roadmap

The central features of the argument in *Making Minds* were clear to me from the beginning: readers might need convincing that conventional education was not good enough; the book would have to be a wide-ranging argument, and one that then indicated where solutions could be found; the processes would need to be described – new methods developed in the social sciences as well as in neuroscience. Applying these methods to education, the book would need to indicate how learning could be, and give a glimpse of the future where making minds would be the norm.

So this book is set out as a journey in stages from where we are now to where we might aim to be. At the start, it may seem a bleak assessment of what is wrong with education, but it becomes more positive. At the beginning, there is a chapter on the state of play in education. The middle of the book interleaves chapters on the educational problems of segregation, prejudice and politics (Chapters 2, 4 and 6) with the emerging solutions (Chapters 3, 5 and 7). The final Chapters (8 and 9) look at the impact of technology and science respectively on the process of making human minds, and the implications for everyone.

Making Minds uses examples to illustrate some of the problems faced in improving how people learn rather than offering an exhaustive catalogue of issues, or detailed examination of any one of them. The book is designed to present a central thesis and to illustrate that thesis by giving readers plenty of food for thought. It focuses on formal education as a starting point, using examples to show the difference between how we want children's education to be and what often really happens. It does not offer a solution to all problems in education, but rather shows how there is the critical mass of people and processes needed to transform our understanding of learning: as with all change in the early stages, this is more about how solutions are being found than what the solutions are.

This book gives readers a glimpse of many different issues. For readers who wish to pursue particular topics, the Notes section at the end of the book offers starting points that are easily accessible and lead to the detailed (and often enormous) literature around some of the topics. I have tried to use free sources available on the internet so that readers can explore issues cheaply and rapidly. I have used some examples from Monkseaton High School where I work to show how real schools and teachers can contribute to the process, without, I hope, suggesting that these are the only solutions. The reliance on BBC News Online for many issues is intentional: it is probably the best free-to-use news site on the internet.

In the end, the message of this book is positive about learning and about people. *Making Minds* is certainly not going to please all its readers all of the time because it deliberately challenges beliefs that many people have held all their lives. It does indicate the way forward, and the logic behind rejecting conventional wisdom. Understanding learning will lead to understanding the creation of minds using rigorous experimental methods, new scientific knowledge and the economic imperative for societies to maximize human potential.

Unlike other animals, humans create new tools

Learning is adapting to the environment, and one of the unique features of people was that they learned to create new tools that helped them adapt. These tools could be physical – as in technology – or understanding – as in knowledge of mathematics and science. People very quickly realized that preserving these tools from one generation to another was vital, and hence learning itself became an increasingly important skill. Somewhat ironically, people did not apply the tools they created to their internal environment – the brain (and it was only in the past few hundred years that they realized it was the brain that was the organ of learning). People continued to learn and transmit their knowledge using techniques created by chance, and these became our conventional wisdom of formal education. Better tools were invented that could be used on learning, such as those in social sciences and, in relation to the brain itself, neuroscience, but these have only rarely been used.

Education is like other aspects of society where the conventional wisdom dominates our actions. J. K. Galbraith pointed out that conventional wisdom was dominant where evidence was not easily available. He argued that in such situations, people were free to have their own theories with no regard to truth, that the dominance of one set of ideas arose from how acceptable those ideas were and that they would then prove very hard to dislodge. This book is written from a specific world view: knowing what to measure, and how to measure it, is a key to beginning the process of moving beyond the conventional wisdom. This is because measurement makes evidence easily available, and conventional wisdom can be confronted – and changed. The social sciences can contribute rigorous experimental techniques using sophisticated statistical methods to this process. In the end, the fundamental principles will arise from scientific research in neuroscience, though at the moment less is known about forming minds – about learning – than any other area of such importance in people's lives.

The analytical tools created in the social sciences (especially economics) can be applied to learning, and it appears that the economics of education may be no different from the economics of the rest of human activity. Steven D. Levitt, the eminent Chicago University professor, has offered a succinct version of economic principles in *Freakonomics* that offers a powerful analytical tool when applied to education:

- Conventional wisdom is often wrong, but teachers, experts and governments persist in copying the mistakes of the past.
- Experts often pursue their own agendas.
- Education is prone to the abuse of political lobbying.
- Knowing what to measure and how to measure it is the key to progress.
- Incentives matter.
- Dramatic improvements can come from simple changes. There are solutions we can put in place.

Education is an increasingly expensive process, and questions need to be asked about how successful it is. Is education effective? Do students gain all the skills and knowledge they need for life? Is education efficient? This is not just a question of money but of the amount of time people spend learning. Is education engaging? The customers – the learners – should come first, and there should be incentives to win their interest and commitment. And what is our aim in education – to create the citizens we wish children to be, or to help them be independent, adaptive learners? Making the minds of our children is not the same as having the right to determine what they think, believe and feel.

As of this moment, scientific analysis of learning has hardly made any impact on education. In contrast, knowledge in the areas of technology and science generally is growing rapidly. As we will see, this knowledge is often quite at odds with the conventional wisdom of education. The scientific understanding of the human brain, and how it works, is beginning to show that learning is not an abstract transmission of knowledge to an infinitely plastic intelligence but a biochemical process with physical limitations.

We are in the midst of a scientific revolution in biochemistry, particularly human biological processes. Discoveries abound; for example, it has been discovered that all people on earth are descendants of only 35 women, and scientists can trace these women back to a single woman alive less than 200,000 years ago through the mitochondrial DNA of thousands of people. Modern science can even manipulate DNA to alter living things. Yet we still do not know the best way to help a child learn to read, or even all the processes in the brain that underlie reading.

Some 200 years ago medicine was in darkness, blundering from one fad to another, as education is now. The solution for medicine was an application of scientific method, combined with a clear process: developing accepted international methodologies for improving knowledge of effective practice, based on rigorous experiments, and sharing them across the world. We can, if we choose, use the same processes to work together to improve learning for every person, starting with learning from each other, looking for what is best in the many educational systems that do exist. Such a process will make learning effective and efficient, creating independent learners who enjoy learning – and it will stop the current waste of children's time and people's potential.

Making Minds is aimed at parents, learners, those in the education industry and those in the wider scientific community. It focuses on children because that is where the process of learning begins. Education systems can be based on the idea that force-feeding human beings a so-called academic diet using methods that are literally centuries old is a good idea. This book makes the case that we can do better. The human mind is, seemingly, impossible to understand, as the trillions of connections that exist in the brain demonstrate. However, we can understand the processes of the human mind, despite this immense complexity. It is a very long journey to embark upon, and one that seems to dwarf attempts to understand the physical universe. As Ramachandran, a leading American neurologist, argued, the quest to understand minds is 'the greatest adventure that our species has ever embarked upon'.

Chapter 1

In the beginning

Educational trial and error

In the beginning

Learning is a science, not an art. Our biology determines how we learn, and how we have evolved to adapt to our environment, yet education systems do not take into account the biological basis of learning.

Consider newborn children. They have to learn to understand the whole world: the space we inhabit; the distance between objects; what people are and who they can trust; how to feed; how to move; how to understand talk, and then to talk; how to move their bodies, to crawl, to walk; to love and be loved. They do all this by sharing our world, our food and our lives. They accomplish all this in two years.

Consider the child in education. They have to learn the skills of school; they have to absorb information about thousands of things that have no immediate relevance to their lives; to read, to write (if they have not learned at home); to learn things only to forget them; to sit for hours in a day and listen to an adult; to try to learn separated from the people they love; and to take tests so they can prove themselves better than other children. They do this separate from our world, our food and our lives. Many children fail to accomplish all these things, even though billions are spent on education systems. This can take up to 20 years of their lives.

Consider the young adult. At the end of formal education, when they launch themselves back into their life, they quickly have to get a job, find a home and make a contribution to the world and themselves. They do this with us: living and working, eating our food and helping to change our world. Most of them succeed. They accomplish all this in about two years.

Education systems are, after all, relatively new. Yet a baby's learning suggests quite a different approach from formal education: for them, learning seems an inborn disposition, a fundamental skill in our species. Education systems, however, still seem unable to take advantage of this inborn disposition. From an evolutionary and biological perspective learning is part of humanity's biological adaptedness. We adapt to our world not only in terms of biological change (over long periods) but also in terms of our ability to learn behaviour. Adaptedness makes us better able to survive and multiply. Evolutionary biologists are quite clear about the significant advantages for a species of social adaptedness.

The transfer of knowledge and skills has changed the human condition. It is directly responsible for humans being the only living thing to escape the biological restrictions on population growth. Language, although not solely a human trait, is a fundamental feature of that ability to transfer knowledge. All these changes are outcomes of an organic, evolutionary process. In contrast, education systems are an attempt to build an abstract, formal process that transfers knowledge. Not surprisingly, education systems are not very successful – yet.

The biological basis of human behaviour is already known in very broad outline. The development of knowledge in neuroscientific, genetic and related sciences is very rapid. In due course we will understand much more, but we should not imagine that the outcome of this research will reinforce conventional wisdom about learning.

Challenges to our conventional wisdom have emerged in some important areas. It appears that human brains are continuing to evolve, possibly with radical implications. There have been recent changes in the DNA associated with brain size. These changes affect genes, where new variations, called 'gene variants', have occurred. At first, only a few people have these new gene variants, but two of these variants emerged roughly at the same time as our social behaviour changed. This has raised the question of a possible connection with our cultural evolution. One of these new gene variants (the 'microcephalin variant') appeared about 50,000 years ago, when humans began to use art and music, religious practices and sophisticated tool-making techniques. For some reason, 70 per cent of us already have this variant – a very rapid spread for a single gene variant. Thus it may have some significant benefits. The other similar genetic change (the 'ASPM gene variant') appeared just 5,800 years ago, when humans started to use agriculture, settled cities and began to use written language more widely. Already 30 per cent of us have this gene variant – and again this rapid spread suggests a genetic change that has significant benefits.

It seems, therefore, that changes in our genes have occurred in parallel with significant changes in our adaptedness. The researchers involved in these discoveries note that these changes have occurred in a very short period, which indicates 'intense selection pressures'. These genetic variants have not been directly linked to intelligence (though there may be links), but the real issue is that the human brain is changing, and that there may be an interaction between genetic change and apparently learned behaviours. The implications of this are profound: have we only begun a process of evolution where interaction with human civilization changes the value (and therefore spread) of genetic variants? If so, revolutions in the knowledge we have and use may affect our evolutionary development through such mechanisms. Whatever the answer, we now know that humans have not stopped evolving, and that the barrier we have always assumed existed between our minds and our physical evolution may, in reality, not exist at all.

Does education make you fat?

The pressures on growing children today may be of a different kind than they were 200 years ago, when hunger and disease were normal, but the pressures are very real.

Things have not turned out as well as predicted 50 years ago when the economists realized that hunger could be eradicated. In *The Affluent Society* Galbraith argued that people in affluent societies would be free from the fear of want. Full production became the goal (though only achieved by want creation – advertising, for example) and education would create a 'New Class' of those that enjoyed their work and an enviable life style. How did long-term economic change really affect children? Galbraith's conviction that an educated New Class would spring up ignored other industrial providers of pleasure in modern society, such as the fast food industry, the entertainment industry and the legal and illegal drugs industries. Education now competes with these other calls upon people's attention. An easy demonstration of these economic realities lies in the answer to a simple question – what are the biggest dangers facing our affluent children? Depending where you live in the world, they could be crime, wars, disease or famine. But in an affluent society the reality is different. The biggest threats to children are commercial products: cigarettes, alcohol and other drugs, cars and food itself. Food is a good example. The growth of the processed food industry and advertising has a marked effect: the industry exploited our food habits, increasing our daily calorie consumption. This is because of our natural inclination to favour high-calorie foods. The consequence of this commercial activity is a strong tendency in every affluent society to become obese.

Obesity has now been described as an epidemic, and the possibility that this generation will be the first generation in which children routinely die before their parents is very real, according to the US Surgeon General. The educational response to the crisis has often been self-serving, promoting conventional wisdom and the institutional educational agenda. Educationalists have quite openly used the danger to young people to seek additional funding for programmes whose failure has been a contributing factor to the rise of obesity: traditional schooling and PE teaching.

Epidemics are marked by rapid increases in disease, and the Surgeon General's report on obesity is able to present this in a very compelling fashion, as shown in Figure 1.1. This epidemic is clearly related to the commercial and industrial approaches to food in the US and other affluent societies. The Surgeon General's report does not attack these economic processes, though it notes that the consumption of huge quantities of high-calorie processed foods is a major contributing factor in the rise of obesity. The media focus has often been on the most obvious examples of processed foods, such as hamburgers. To be fair to the McDonald's restaurants of the world, shopping in Wal-Mart stores in America can be just as dangerous: huge quantities of processed food items are offered at discount prices, but only when purchased in volume. It hardly encourages good eating habits.

The attempt to use this epidemic by pressure groups is instructive. For example, Lynn Swann, Chairman of the President's Council on Physical Fitness and Sports, notes that: '400,000 people a year die from conditions related to physical inactivity combined with poor diet. Only smoking kills more people – 435,000 people a year. The gap is closing fast.' But Swann then goes on to assert that: 'a remedy already exists, [with] no costs except commitment and determination. That medical miracle is daily physical activity.' Swann does not challenge the economic powers that be: to mention the commercial food companies, their advertising and the political power of a multi-billion dollar industry, and link these to the pernicious effect of 'poor diet' would be too dangerous, perhaps. The 'medical miracle' would not work on its own, but it would increase funding for the institutional interests Swann represents.

A factor that has never been mentioned is society's role in children's inactivity. For example, what has made children sit down for hours a day, focus

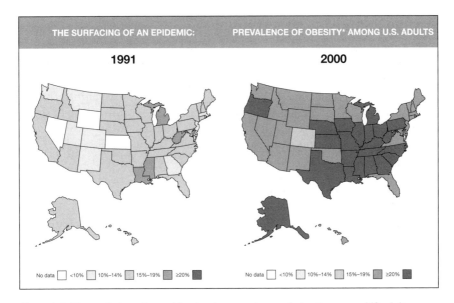

Figure 1.1 The surfacing of an epidemic: the prevalence of obesity among US adults

Source: Behavioral Risk Factor Surveillance System (BRFSS)
Note: Obesity is defined as approximately 30 pounds overweight. BFRSS uses self-report height and weight to calculate obesity; self-reported data may underestimate obesity prevalence.

their attention on just one thing, and isolates them from normal activities with their families and peers? School. School usually keeps children inactive at desks for many more hours than television does (though, interestingly, children who like learning at school usually like learning from television). Schools fail to challenge the commercial food providers, as well as providing poor food. Rapidly evolving new business practices (such as in the fast food industry) combined with little or no guidance from schools and parents may have produced a literally lethal combination. The epidemic has evoked a powerful response by government, at least in terms of reports and sports-based projects, but little significant headway has been made on the underlying problems.

Galbraith's vision of increasing numbers of people living a healthy and fulfilled life, shaped through high educational achievement, has been undermined by economic forces from those that created affluent societies: industries. Our society is one in which fast food, cars, drugs, cigarettes, commercial products of every kind and non-stop distraction from the entertainment industry are available for everyone. Education will not be able to compete, unless it is engaging – and forthright about the limitations and dangers of a life based on consumption. In crude terms, children have economic choices that include healthy life styles, exercise and learning – or gratification through commercial products. No one should be surprised at consequences such as drug abuse or obesity.

A child's intellectual potential

There are, however, economic forces that encourage children to succeed in education. Before turning to this, it is useful to consider the growing academic expectations of children and how realistic they are. There is no obvious limit to how intelligent children can become. In the past it has been argued that an individual's ability to learn is limited and largely fixed by birth, race or social position. Theoretically, it now looks as if most children can achieve to a very high level. There are signs that people are actually becoming more intelligent: there apparently has been a significant increase in the IQ scores of children worldwide in the last generation.

If one examines the history of exceptionally able people, it is possible to see two types of explanation of why they are so able. Again, a historically popular view was that genius or exceptional ability was a question of an inborn gift. In contrast with this view, it is becoming clear that the answer may lie in the amount of time a child spends in a certain activity. Mozart is an example of a genius created through a rigid regimen focused on a single skill. In a recent biography Mozart's passionate need for affection and seeming obsession with music are linked directly to his father's focus on his commercial value as a prodigy. His father's fixation meant that Mozart had to devote most of his waking hours to music. A similar rigid regime, but in a school, forced Christopher Marlowe, the Elizabethan playwright, to focus on literature to the exclusion of almost everything else. Of course, it is not as simple as this: neither Bach nor Shakespeare was a product of such restrictive upbringing. Application may make a huge difference, but it is probably not the only factor.

One conclusion is that it is possible to raise children in such a way that they become exceptionally able in at least one area. We have yet to understand this process, or to apply it in learning. The dreams of parents for their children to achieve great things are, therefore, justified; their tragedy is that, at the moment, they are unlikely to be realized.

A child's economic potential

There are clear economic incentives that encourage children to succeed in education. Young people earn more money if they are educated to a high standard, and this is a driving force behind parents' desire to see their children do well. There is, of course, a tendency to think of this process as a competition against other people's children rather than an attempt to universally raise levels of achievement, as education is another social indicator of a successful life.

Most people believe in the value of education in principle, even if it is only the economic value of education. Although they may think education has improved, they still criticize what happens in schools and universities. This suggests that they believe education is a good thing in economic terms, but are disappointed with the effectiveness of the education they and their children have received. This collective perception is a fair assessment, and raises the question: why does this happen?

Parents want their children to be healthy, happy and successful, and education is seen as a means to economic success. Education seems to offer a clear measure for parents – their children are graded in relation to other children, and they can judge how well their children are performing as developing economic citizens. The world judges children by their educational achievement, and there is a clear link between these education levels and their future financial success. There is no doubt that university (or, as they will have it in the US, college) education makes an economic difference to people: in broad terms, having a degree is worth a million dollars to any person who has one, and no parent can ignore that. If a child can succeed in education, then they are likely to earn more money, live longer and see their own children succeed.

As education is a way of improving the life chances of children, rich parents will try to buy a better educational experience. Richer countries spend more on education, and can have better educational outcomes. Despite that, more poor people have improved their social and economic status through education than through any other way. This has some interesting implications: if wealth could buy better education, then the educational gap between rich and poor would always increase as a result of 'buying' educational success, but it does not. The educational gap between rich and poor children is usually decreased in schools that do not charge fees. However, if there are high costs, this is not always true: in England the recent expansion in university education has benefited the better off, and this has decreased social mobility.

The comforting implication of this could be that schools improve poor people's life chances because you cannot buy education or natural intelligence. The alternative explanation is more likely to be true: rich people (and rich countries) do not know what they are doing in education, and therefore no amount of money will buy them an education that preserves their social advantages – that is, until someone discovers how to create and sell educational advantage. In other words, education systems, schools and universities do not guarantee success. So parents are right to be unhappy about schools and universities – they do not necessarily deliver educational advantage.

Of course, education does not just occur in the formal education system of schools and universities. It occurs in homes, in social situations and in the daily work of every person. This vision of education occurring all around us might sound idealistic. Perhaps it should be thought of as a warning: if education is not good enough, then we are all responsible for that shortcoming: parents, peers, education systems and society itself.

The economy benefits from children's education

Employers pay more to young people who have achieved highly because they believe they are more valuable. Companies, and the economy generally, appear to benefit from high educational outcomes. In business there is also a belief that the transfer of knowledge and information is an important part of making profits: we are in a knowledge or information society.

This knowledge society may or may not exist, but the indicators are that it does. Certainly the knowledge society is an accepted theory in the US, Europe and the OECD (Organization for Economic Cooperation and Development) countries. If it is true, education is the next economic hurdle: how are we going to match the exponential growth in science and technology if we cannot improve the performance of people? This has led to deep concerns in some affluent countries about how to raise the educational level of their citizens. The UK, lagging behind other similar countries in the percentage of graduates in the workforce, simply set an artificial target of 50 per cent of all young people going to university. In the US, where this target has already been reached, many worry that the quality of degrees is becoming lower, and increasingly students find that there is the pressure to obtain postgraduate qualifications.

This panic (or appropriate action if you prefer) to raise the perceived level of educational achievement has led to simplistic visions that translate higher levels of education as equivalent to better economic performance. International think tanks propose visions of teaching changing, information society growing and the population becoming better workers through the development of education, leading to more advanced economies. The economic and educational dynamics of advanced economies must be more complex than this, though – perhaps – the underlying principles may be correct.

There are problems with such simple solutions. Even assuming that the number of students achieving degree standard can be increased (albeit slowly), the relentless advances in technology and science require higher and higher levels of expertise. For all the hype about improving education, simple models based on slow improvements in degree outcomes will fail to keep pace with changes in the world. The solution to this very real problem is not clear, but the necessity for greater efficiency, so that people can reach higher levels of educational attainment more quickly (and cheaply), is apparent. The lengthening time that education systems now take to prepare children for the modern world, and the growth of the post-work population, makes the current approach unsustainable: there would be too few people actually working. This is not the message that the education industry wants to broadcast: it continues to encourage society, business and individuals to spend longer and longer in formal, often full-time education. There is a very considerable incentive for educational institutions to promote such behaviour: they make more money. Societies are already facing problems in meeting the demands for more years of formal education and many advanced economies can indicate potential dangers if this trend is not curtailed. For example, Japan has an ageing population, a rapidly falling birth rate and high educational demands. Suicide of Japanese school children has been an acknowledged problem. The pressures on young people to succeed are intense, but prosperity means there is, on some levels, no need to work at all. The young adults who stay in their rooms, living entirely off their parents' income and refusing to work or take part in society – the Hikikomori – show this is true. There is no compelling incentive for them to rejoin society and its pressures. The rest of us may face similar problems soon.

The acceleration of knowledge

A rapid increase in the understanding of the world in the last 100 years means there are greater pressures on education. Education is not alone in facing these problems: this acceleration of humanity's knowledge is faced by scientists, the technology industry and society as a whole. The developments in science are increasingly difficult to manage for the scientists themselves. Even the speed at which innovations move from research to implementation is accelerating. The developments in genetic engineering, nanotechnology and environmental research are already having a profound impact on the way people understand and interact with the world.

The number of scientific papers published has forced scientists to develop new approaches to the sharing of research outcomes. Jon Kleinberg at Cornell University illustrates some of the new issues and approaches of the scientific community:

> the Internet is bringing about a much broader evolution in the way scientists work and communicate. Information and value increasingly lies not just in the published article but in relationships between articles, in the links among authors and papers, and in less formal communication among users and communities through Weblogs (or 'blogs'), listservs, home pages and other sources on the Web.

Another consequence of the increase in scientific knowledge is the growing number of projects involving scientists in different countries. This inventive responsiveness to change is in stark contrast to education systems. This might be because in education systems the approach to transferring knowledge is not yet successfully responding to the need to stay abreast of knowledge – never mind working together to share knowledge.

A specific area where there is very rapid growth in knowledge is information technology (IT). Unlike technological progress in general, there has been an attempt to quantify the speed of development in IT. Moore's Law is a well-known theory that predicted that the number of transistors in each integrated circuit would double every 18 months, and it has proved to be an accurate projection (see Figure 1.2). It also gives a measure of the processing power of computers and, by implication, the information-handling potential of computers.

The simplicity of the graph is deceiving: in 1970 you would have needed a million PCs linked together to match the power of one of today's personal computers. Another way to look at it is to consider the number of transistors: 30 years ago, computers had only 1,000; now there are well over a billion in small silicon chips in an ordinary PC.

The important point is not that technology is improving. It is that the potential power of technology to process information is doubling every 18 months. Seen as a mechanism for transferring knowledge, the development of ICT (information and communication technology) parallels the impact of writing and printing on knowledge transfer, but a thousand years of progress is being compressed into a few decades. It is already reaching most people on earth – either directly (by having access to computing or the internet) or indirectly through ICT-supported change.

Programmes and content on ICT systems are, however, little more than a digitalization of human thought or understanding. One example is language: computers work through such a code. For example, 'http' at the beginning of Web addresses is a reminder of the code or language used for the Web:

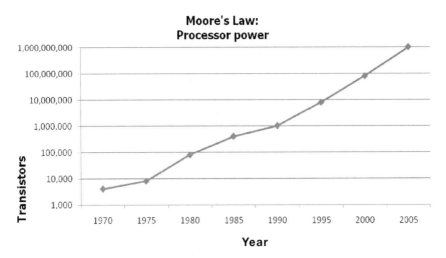

Figure 1.2 Moore's Law

Hypertext Markup Language (HTML). This language allows computers everywhere to understand the same instructions. It is perhaps a mark of the progress in this field that in just a few years a language has been invented and consequently taken up in hundreds of millions of machines across the world.

Let us return for a moment to the million billion neural connections in a human brain. The sheer complexity of the networks in the brain seems to defy any attempt to discover the physical mechanisms of thought. This may no longer be the case. The combination of advanced scientific methods, mathematics and computing is beginning to solve problems that appeared impossible a decade ago. The behaviour of quarks – one of the particles that are the basis of all matter – has always been a mystery. A mathematical model of their behaviour within a complex system was created and fed into computers, and calculated for every part of the system, tracking the behaviours of particles that are almost impossible to track in experiments. In this case, the calculations took months on the world's fastest supercomputers. At the same time, detailed experiments were carried out using particle accelerators. The approach of matching mathematical modelling and experimental data worked to reveal how quarks do behave. Such combined approaches offer a glimpse of the methods that we could use for understanding activity within the human brain. We are used to such scientific and technological breakthroughs, but why not in education? This is because education has yet to create a process that leads to radical improvements or even one that fully embraces science and technology.

Can education change?

Education systems need a revolution. The acceleration of knowledge has made this more urgent. Unfortunately, educational institutions can be remarkably resistant to change. An example is the university admissions system in England. Universities admit students before their examination results are known, so only predictions from schools are available. This unsatisfactory situation is made worse by poor interviewing, no tests of potential (similar to the Scholastic Aptitude Tests in the US) and no rigorous quality control of the process. In fact, admission to English universities can be a bit of a lottery.

Laura Spence was one of my truly exceptional students: talented, funny, exceptionally bright, focused, thoughtful, very principled and able to relate to almost everyone. She applied to universities in the UK and the US. She was offered a place in all but one of them, and was one of ten British students to win Harvard scholarships in her year. Oxford managed to get it wrong, and not offer her a place. In a regional newspaper, *The Journal*, I argued the obvious point: Oxford rejecting such an exceptional student was a worrying sign of major weaknesses in the admissions system. I was later told by a national newspaper reporter that I was the 132nd person to complain about English admissions problems in 2000 alone.

Oxford admissions are handled by the small segments of the university that are called colleges. After my complaint, the college responded very aggressively indeed, attempting a defence of the indefensible in the national press. It was difficult to understand such foolish actions without an insider's view. *The Oxford Student* came closest to explaining what had really happened in an article appropriately entitled 'Imagine if they did it to you':

> Magdalen College is fighting to recover from a public relations disaster after the release of an interview report on the state school candidate who failed to gain a place there, but went on to scoop a scholarship to Harvard. A copy of the report on Laura Spence's interview for a place to study Medicine was sent [by the college] to the *Daily Mail*, *The Journal* and *The Today Programme* [BBC] on Monday. [Laura Spence] was rejected despite her ten A*s at GCSE, straight As predicted at A-level, distinction in an Open University Mathematics course and Grade 8 violin. The report – which would normally be kept confidential – notes that Laura was 'v. nice' . . . A spokesman for the University of Oxford made it clear that it was not their policy to discuss individual cases and that this was a college matter. But he agreed that Magdalen had 'dug themselves a bit of a hole there'.
>
> (*The Oxford Student*: 18 May 2000)

The public relations disaster had become a catastrophe: *The Times* ran an editorial comparing Oxford's problems with Cambridge's success in attracting sponsored student places in partnership with Bill Gates. Shortly afterwards, Gordon Brown, then Chancellor of the Exchequer, said Laura's rejection was 'an absolute disgrace', no doubt worried by the economic consequences of elite British students going to, and possibly staying in, the US. The likelihood that the Conservative opposition would be forced to defend elitism in education might have been an additional incentive for the Chancellor to stray from the economy to education.

Laura's story became a national debate and an international news story. There was huge support for her, venom from some, and even some humour. *The Guardian* ran a story about ten possible marriage partners for Prince William and included Laura, but noted that: 'for someone whose name has become synonymous with a crusade against elitism, marrying the next king isn't a wholly obvious next move.' The BBC turned the battle of Laura's admission into a rout when it exclusively revealed notes from her interview that suggested clear prejudice against her background. *The Washington Post* seemed to sum up the external view of the Laura Spence row in an article entitled 'Class, not classes, keeps a bright British student out of Oxford':

> Spence has suddenly been cast as a victim in a furious national argument about discrimination in education . . . on grounds that strike many as downright snobbery toward community high schools and their graduates.
>
> As with most of the debates that really get the blood running here, the question revolves around an essential element of British life – social class. In a society that still pays considerable deference to inherited wealth, titles and status, the old school ties of upper-crust British boarding schools such as Eton and Harrow evidently still play a role in Oxbridge admissions.
>
> Spence's defenders argue that her problem with Oxford was that her school in Whitley Bay, outside Newcastle, is a 'comprehensive.' That's the British term for a neighborhood public high school that you can go to without taking an entrance exam. Spence's grades and standardized test scores were top-notch; her downfall came when she traveled here for an admissions interview with an Oxford don, or professor.
>
> In notes made public last week, the don described her as 'outstandingly intelligent' but judged that she would not fit in at Oxford because 'as with other comprehensive school pupils, [she is] low in confidence and [it is] difficult to draw her out of herself.'
>
> (*The Washington Post*: 1 June 2000)

It is, perhaps, easier to judge the consequences of the Laura Spence debate from the long-term outcomes than from the short-term rhetoric. The UK government put pressure on the university admissions system to reform itself. This, combined with the media interest, forced universities to reveal data about admissions that showed high-ranked universities were not admitting state school students in proportion to their success at A level. This was followed by details about state and fee-paying children's admission into each college at Oxford, which showed that in the university, overall, only 53 per cent were from state schools – clearly a much lower figure than it should be. The colleges within Oxford had to reveal for the first time the proportion of state school children they accepted, and it varied from only 40 per cent to nearly 75 per cent – a huge range that appeared to have no rational justification (see table below). Admissions were not really dependent upon grades, but upon the colleges and their admissions process and personnel. Only colleges such as Mansfield reflected an approximation to a realistic assessment. Other high-ranked universities were revealed to have similar problems, though not as extreme as Oxford's.

Not all the blame for these inequalities lies at the door of the universities. Recently it has emerged that the predictions of A level results from the schools themselves are clearly biased too. Only 45 per cent of A level predictions from schools are accurate. Wealthier children get higher predictions, while poor children are given lower predictions. This admissions process is one of the contributing factors to England's unique combination of widening university participation and at the same time increasing social inequalities in educational outcomes.

English universities now have to try and reach targets for state and fee-paying students, as well as narrow the gap between middle-class and poorer students. Oxford and other elite universities were given more money to try to attract a larger number of applicants from state schools – and advertise their institution – and the government set up an independent admissions watch-dog. Oxford still fails to hit its admissions targets, and its colleges have recently fought off the university's attempts to reform their admissions processes. More important, England's admissions system itself remains unreformed:

Table 1.1 Offers made to state school and fee-paying school applicants by Oxford colleges

Oxford colleges (highest and lowest 6 only shown)	Offers to state school applicants	Offers to fee-paying school applicants
Oriel	40.4	59.6
St Edmund Hall	42.2	57.8
Brasenose	44.2	55.8
Trinity	44.4	55.6
Pembroke	44.9	55.1
Magdalen	46.2	53.8
Colleges average	53.6	46.4
Hertford	61.3	38.7
Merton	61.4	38.6
Keble	65.3	34.7
Wadham	66.2	33.8
St John's	69.9	30.1
Mansfield	74.6	25.4

Source: BBC News Online: 4 August 2000

predictions of grades are still used, there are no national tests for potential, and rigorous systems for equal access are not yet in place.

Laura Spence has, however, changed the conventional wisdom about admissions to English universities. There is now an acceptance that things must change, and things are now openly said, albeit years later, that were never said so publicly before.

> Universities might as well toss a coin as interview prospective students, the head of an admissions inquiry told MPs. Professor Steven Schwartz told the Commons education select committee many interviews were unstructured chats. 'These are the type of interviews that take place at some of our most ancient universities and the reliability of these interviews is zero,' he said.
>
> (BBC News Online: 25 November 2004)

Equally damning were the comments from Princeton's Dean of Admissions, who simply said that some admissions decisions at Oxford were wrong. Given the inadequacy of England's admissions system, this remark probably applies to every university.

Is there any light at the end of the tunnel?

The problems of education in a changing world illustrate the power of Levitt's economic analysis of social behaviour in *Freakonomics*. Educational conventional wisdom is often wrong: it is based on tradition, with theories adopted with no regard to their truth and a complete lack of a sound methodology. This is shown in education systems in many ways: in the belief that a knowledge society means more people should simply spend more time in education or in the assumption that universities and teachers are never biased. As in many areas of life, incentives and self-interest matter to individual children, societies and educational institutions. Experts, organizations and governments often pursue their own agenda at the expense of better solutions: the conflict between children's health and commercialism suggests that educationalists and governments often approach such issues with the sword of truth firmly in its scabbard.

Addressing failures in education systems will hinge in large part on knowing what to measure and how to measure it. Without some kind of measurement, people will hold to popular theories, and organizations and individuals will rely on lobbying, not evidence. The conventional wisdom tends to remain dominant where evidence is not easily available. This was true in university admissions in England – many suspected that there was bias and inequality, but it was only with the emergence of data linking admissions to the background of students, and the variation between predicted grades and real performance, that a clear picture of admissions favouring the well-off was revealed. The obesity epidemic was allowed to grow unchecked until a number of authoritative reports tracked the trends and demonstrated the rapid rise in the number of overweight individuals.

The better understanding that emerges from good data does not necessarily make anything happen. Conventional wisdom can be very hard to challenge, and the role of the media is important. Bringing data to the attention of the public – whether on global warming, obesity or university admissions – requires publicity if that information is to make the conventional wisdom unacceptable and create a more informed view. Institutions continue to fight change if it might damage their interests, as the protracted conflict between tobacco companies and the scientific community attests.

The conventional wisdom is that education is different from ordinary human activity in business and most public services because it is benign, well meaning and progressive. The evidence suggests the opposite: like all human activity, education is beset with segregation, prejudice and politics. The effectiveness, efficiency and human engagement in education are, at present, barely acceptable. Self-interest and conventional wisdom are the major factors for individuals and institutions. At the same time, good education has a huge amount to offer: it is a valuable experience, and one that is fundamental to modern life.

Like the rest of human activity, education is now facing an exponential change in science and technology, and even the economic process of globalization. As educational consumers, students are already responding to this changing environment. They are more confident in accepting the challenge of moving from one country to another, from one culture to another. As students are increasingly being charged for their higher education, they are now more aware of the overall cost and are looking for value for money.

The Laura Spence controversy demonstrated again that much of educational practice is unjustifiable tradition, but there can be fierce resistance to change. Institutional self-interest is not just a barrier to change, but more fundamentally it suggests education is often not focusing on being effective (or efficient and engaging). This is because educationalists often see as their real customers not the students but their paymasters – the government or, for fee-paying institutions, the parents. We must hope that another political solution is not forthcoming: challenging conventional wisdom in a political arena is never easy, and this cannot be the way to improve things – it has failed too many times.

If conventional wisdom represents the way people believe education functions, then an economic and scientific analysis represents how education really does function in today's world. This might suggest that there is no light at the end of the tunnel. I believe this is too bleak a view. Most of the people who work in education are desperate to improve it; most teachers and lecturers are gifted and humane; parents go to great lengths to help their children; and good learning experiences are a joy for children themselves. Yet those people are constrained by education systems based on traditions and embroiled in political complications. It is the framework in which education operates that must change, moving from conventional wisdom to knowledge based on sound data and experiment. Knowledge about learning processes based on experiment is possible, practical and affordable, but the first step is to explore the barriers to progress.

Chapter 2

Education as segregation

Source: The National Archives and Records Administration, US, 1963

Education is the most powerful weapon which you can use to change the world.

Nelson Mandela

Educational segregation reflects segregation in society

In South Africa apartheid ensured that it was difficult for black children to benefit from education, and there was a considerable funding gap between black and white schools and universities. Despite the end of apartheid, the consequences of apartheid continue to plague South African schools. The restructuring of South African universities, starting with educational reforms from 1987, took many years to address the institutional boundaries that had been created in a segregated past. The impact of segregation on individuals continues long after legal segregation has disappeared. It is not just an individual's negative attitudes, poor self-image or sectarianism but economic disadvantage perpetuated from generation to generation. Any educational benefits for children can take over a generation to have a significant impact on society. Mandela is right to see education as a key to improving the world, but it tends to work very slowly.

[Education systems embody the prejudices of society. Overt and covert segregation has been common in schools and universities, and in many ways remains so] In the US, South Africa and elsewhere, education institutions have been overtly separated on racial lines; in most countries there are divisions on religious lines; and all countries have some form of segregation by wealth, or class, or ability, or location – or a combination of these. Perhaps the most pervasive segregation is by nation: education systems reflect political systems as well as being controlled by them.]

Education segregates by institutions as well since there are many different kinds: nursery school, first school, primary school, middle school, high school, all-age school, technical school, military school, dance school, monastery, junior college, further education college, gymnasium, international school, fee-paying school, Catholic school, Jewish school, Buddhist school, Sikh school, schooling at home, and any one of literally thousands of other alternative institutions all operating differently, not to mention a bewildering range of universities and colleges. These organizations have often been created by chance, historical precedent or political fiat, and are very difficult to change because for most institutions their first aim is survival, not improving learning. They tend to strongly defend their organization, and can want to maintain their links to the past, to traditions and to the community.

The consequences for children can be quite dramatic. For example, in England there was a historical division for children at 11 years old between grammar schools and secondary modern schools, with most children going to secondary moderns. The division was segregation based on an inadequate test called the eleven-plus (and some children were not even allowed to attempt the test). Secondary modern children were given a less challenging curriculum – for example, some 15-year-old girls were taught how to clean toilets. In 1973 this division was removed by creating all-in comprehensive schools, and this caused a political debate that still continues, largely ignored by the rest of the world where such an educational division never occurred in the first place. The consequence was that children's education improved. Recently, German education has also been under pressure to reform its selective system, having successfully managed to ignore the lessons from England for over 30 years.

Education can produce economic as well as social advantages, so parents often try to use the education system to advantage their children. It is not surprising to find that richer, more influential parents are more likely to succeed in using education in this way. Thus education can be segregated into supposedly 'separate but equal' institutions through direct political control but also through covert parental actions (such as buying an expensive house near a 'good' school). Some institutional segregation is so engrained into our thinking about education as to be almost invisible. For example, schools are fundamentally different institutions from universities in almost every country, and the age of transition is about 18. There is no obvious logic in having this rigid dividing line between universities as research-based institutions and schools as solely teaching institutions.

Universities, too, reflect the prejudices of society, though many are predicated on seemingly egalitarian principles. There are social differences between universities that can be very marked, but the real segregation that universities almost universally perpetuate is one based on perceived academic ability. The core assumption is that only certain people should be allowed to attempt a university degree. Industrial societies have seen the percentage of children going to university rocket from less than 5 per cent to over 50 per cent in the last 50 years, which radically alters that assumption – yet it remains firmly in place. Most universities take this much further, by trying to identify the academic qualities of applicants in order to select by ability. Indeed, if selection based on perceived academic ability has bedevilled education, the fault lies at the door of universities. The concept of the right of children to a university education has not, as yet, become established in any country.

Some forms of segregation at universities are unintentional, others are not. For example, universities in both the US and England have been accused of allowing racial segregation to grow in their institutions:

> American universities reflect American society – where you do have completely segregated communities. Our fear would be that this is happening here as well . . . [The Higher Education Statistics Agency]

figures on the ethnicity of students in higher education show a disturbing racial divide among universities.

(*The Guardian*: 3 January 2006)

Other forms of division – for example by parents' income and class – though well known, do not always evoke such headlines.

Education institutions do try to segregate themselves from society – the ivory tower syndrome is a very real one. This can be a real impediment to improvement as such institutions are less inclined to look at new organizational approaches used in business, technology and science. In some Spanish universities candidates in degree examinations who memorize long quotations from their lecturers are rewarded, not penalized. This rote memory skill is, at best, totally irrelevant in modern industries. Thus the current organization of education often prevents learning as well as enabling it. We are blinded by local history, systems that have been created piecemeal over the centuries, and traditions that separate learners from communities rather than drawing them together. These systems are self-perpetuating, and often have little relationship to economic or societal needs.

The consequence of educational provision that depends on country, religion or other factors is that learning experiences are coloured by the education system children find themselves in. Children's rights to education are limited the moment they step into a school. This is despite the many people who work in education systems who are devoted to helping learners achieve their full potential. Nevertheless, the impact of the education system as a whole is often negative: memories of school are often of boredom, frustration and failure, and differences in the educational experience can impact on the rest of a child's life. Education sometimes aspires to right social injustices, but in reality it often reinforces them.

The measurement myth

The number of qualifications and assessments in education is probably in the millions. The mania to judge children, schools, teachers and education systems by numbers, letters and bits of paper goes far beyond the process of selection for university. These measurements are used to categorize and group children in thousands of different ways, creating all sorts of segregation within classrooms, schools and society, especially employment. The use of these assessments is so pervasive that such measurements are often mistaken for the central purpose of education. Yet educational assessments as a measure of real learning are, at the moment, basically myths: measurement is at best only approximate and almost universally aimed at categorizing people into successes – or failures. Of course, these measurements have been created by education systems to justify their existence, their system and – at times – their income. A piece of paper that says 'Diploma', 'Honours Degree', 'General Certificate of Education in Combined Science' or 'Scholastic Aptitude Test' is only a piece of paper. It is surprising how much influence such pieces of paper have come to have in societies.

To many parents and children education appears to be about collecting grades, levels or names that indicate a supposed set of accomplishments or skills. Unlike the different currencies that are in use in the world, there is no useful exchange rate to indicate what these qualifications are worth in a different context. At least with money you can find out what yen are worth in dollars, or roubles are worth in euros. And you know that each dollar is the same as every other dollar. In education this is not true. Institutions attended are thought to indicate ability more accurately than qualifications, and there are seen to be hard subjects and easy ones. Cambridge University has recently made it clear that many A levels are not suitable – usually ones with the word 'Studies' in the title. Governments and the education industry like to argue that standards are improving. There are rather embarrassing examples of manipulation of the figures: in England, grades in examinations at 16 and 18 increased slightly each year over many years. Of course English education was not improving steadily over all these years, and a simpler explanation for the rise exists. Examinations boards' income depended on schools choosing their qualifications. Schools' income depended on parents thinking results were improving: so schools would switch examinations if things did not go well. But no one could afford to let society at large think the examinations were easier. There was a clear incentive for examinations to be made easier – but gradually – and so, miraculously, the grades crept up.

Governments have been keen to use qualifications to measure the success of teachers, schools or education systems – but rarely seek failure. This puts pressure on the system, from qualification inflation to cheating. A famous though extreme example of this is the cheating in tests in Chicago schools where teachers gave children the right answers. Unfortunately for the teachers, this was cleverly detected by researchers who noticed that all students in some classes were getting a long series of difficult answers correct after failing to answer easy questions. Yet all these issues about measurement do not alter the fact that the dumbing-down argument is basically incorrect. It has been a theme in all societies for people to complain that things are not as good as they used to be. The evidence suggests otherwise: the percentage of the world's children in schools across the world has continued to rise, the percentage of people with degrees is rising, and literacy levels are rising, though all are improving more slowly than is sometimes claimed.

Qualifications have negative effects in many ways. Inspections or government judgements based on examination performance are usually unjustifiable, yet they can have a powerful impact inside schools and universities. Schools trying to improve examination performance may concentrate on examination practice only, overestimate the quality of school-based assessments or simply cheat on results. Universities trying to climb league tables may focus on published papers at the expense of quality research. Current measurements are destructive because they focus on very limited aspects of learning, distort the focus of learning and give a false sense of precision.

The autism 'epidemic'

Educational assessments are used in such a way that they can often influence the whole of a person's life, income and social status. Some of the more dramatic impacts of educational measurement can be seen in negative accreditations, an area of greater turbulence, controversy, ignorance – and myth.

Autism – one of those negative accreditations – is at the centre of a media storm because of a huge increase in the number of children diagnosed as being autistic: an epidemic seems to be affecting children. 'Autism' began in 1948 as a proposed syndrome for children with very great social and communication problems. It has grown in popularity as a description. Increases of 100 per cent in a few years are not uncommon in developed countries. In California it was even reported that autism cases had grown by over 700 per cent in just 16 years.

This huge growth in reported cases led to research into the cause. People searched for something that was affecting so many children, something new in children's environment (to account for the apparent sudden surge in autism). Vaccines were a common target because they were introduced about the time that autism became a popular description. In the UK, the combined MMR (measles, mumps and rubella) vaccine was blamed, in the US, a mercury-based vaccination ingredient. Other suspects were allergies, viral infections and antibiotics. Yet all was not as it seemed. The warning signs came as research in many countries (such as Denmark) suggested there might be no link between vaccines and autism. Pressure groups were still formed by concerned parents, and educational experts called for the withdrawal of MMR or changes in the vaccines in the US. The number of diagnoses of autism continued to climb. In the US, politicians became involved.

In 2003 *The Wall Street Journal*, the world's leading business newspaper, challenged the supposed links to vaccines, condemning the 'ugly legal and political spat that has spilled into Congress'. It also pointed to the potential threat to the vaccine programmes: 'like night follows day, the dispute has also brought in the trial lawyers' with 'billion-dollar suits' against vaccine companies. There were threats to children too. The danger *The Wall Street Journal* identified was that parents were becoming frightened and not vaccinating their children against potentially deadly diseases. In the UK, leading experts had also warned that children were at risk because of similar parental fears. Autistic children themselves suffered because research trying to prove over and over that there was no link with vaccines hampered real research into the causes of autistic behaviours.

The Wall Street Journal's editorial brought a storm of protest. One letter sent to the editor even claimed the article was 'a sick act of terrorism'. As in the UK, parents and some autism campaigners reacted angrily to any questioning of their preferred cause for the autism epidemic. But there has never been an autism epidemic. There has been no sudden growth in the number of children with autism in California or anywhere else. It has only seemed as if there was an epidemic. A recent survey of the evidence in *The New Scientist* concluded: 'in actual fact, there is no increase at all'.

How could such an 'epidemic' appear to be real, when it was not? There were real problems in assessment, as there is no biochemical or genetic test – only judgements from the behaviour of children. The lack of physiological measures was linked to changes in the definition of autism and a consequent growth of less severe autism cases (children with some milder symptoms). For example, the educational experts' new criteria in 2000 applied to 1970 data on autism would cause a ten-fold increase in the number of autistic children. In simple terms, the measurement changed to include more children. Awareness in parents and educationalists of symptoms increased referrals. It had reached the tipping point in education systems.

There were even very clear incentives for parents, educationalists and experts to diagnose children as autistic. The stigma once attached to parents of autistic children had all but disappeared: in California, cases of 'mental retardation' fell as cases of less severe autism rose – it was a more acceptable form of need. Parents with autistic children received more help from services for their child – in or out of school. Education services for autistic children received more funding. Experts got more support.

In the whole saga, the only epidemic was of autism experts: there once were only 10 in the US, now there are over 2,000 – a 20,000 per cent increase. The whole process did, however, cause real harm. In America, the issue became highly politicized when lawyers began lawsuits against vaccine manufacturers:

> Congress tried to fix this by including a liability provision in homeland security legislation a year ago. But three Northeast Republican Senators – Olympia Snowe, Susan Collins and Lincoln Chafee – demanded it be taken out until Congress could have a full airing of the thimerosal-autism issue. The Senators haven't yet honored their side of that deal.
>
> Perhaps that's because if they did their position would be exposed as scientifically untenable. The claim is that thimerosal, an organic mercury compound, can cause neurodevelopmental disorders. But study after study has shown that there is simply no such link.
>
> (*The Wall Street Journal*: 29 December 2003)

The negative press coverage of vaccines had an effect on parents. In the UK, *The Sunday Times* report 'Schoolboy, 13, dies as measles makes a comeback' did not just focus on the first death from measles in the UK since the introduction of the measles vaccine, but the wider issues. It reported that there were already 100 measles cases in 2006, when there had only been 77 in the whole of the previous year. Professor David Elliman, consultant in community child health at St George's Hospital, was quoted as saying the MMR vaccine was a necessity for parents: 'there is no justification for leaving children unprotected'. The report makes sombre reading:

> Following the introduction of MMR in 1988, immunisation against measles among children at age two rose from about 75% to 92%, bringing hopes that in developed countries measles would be eradicated in the way smallpox has been worldwide. However, this success was badly damaged following research by Dr Andrew Wakefield . . . In the late 1990s he claimed to have found evidence linking MMR first to inflammatory bowel disease and then to autism . . . MMR take-up slumped as low as 73% . . . In the past year rates have edged upwards [when this paper disclosed that] when Wakefield made his claims, he was funded by lawyers who had employed him to build a case against the vaccine.
>
> (*The Sunday Times*: 2 April 2006)

The educational experts who championed the growth of autism – and fuelled worries about vaccines – no doubt now reflect on the consequences of their actions. The educational experts who saw the importance of autism and supported vaccines as a vital tool in protecting children's health no doubt bemoan the weakness of educational measurement.

Is education an uncontrolled experiment?

Education is the world's largest uncontrolled experiment on people because it is a systematic attempt to modify their adaptation to the environment, to change the way they think and act – yet there is no scientific basis for these systems and their impact, nor is there exploration of alternatives. The contrast between learning at home and other more natural social situations on the one hand, and formal education on the other, is striking.

How did schools arise in the first place? The nurturing, learning function of the family or social group is taken over by a formal system, originally for a vocational purpose: the Egyptians training scribes; endless religions training religious functionaries; governments training accountants, tax collectors and lawyers; crafts and the military training 'raw recruits'. In effect, as societies grew, education developed as a form of training in organizations. Another perspective would see formal education as a form of child care, the family unit outsourcing long-term learning to a system. Teaching became a job with regular hours and pay.

Whatever the specific origins, the consequences are clear: the immediate bonds within a family are replaced by tutors, boarding schools, indentures, monasteries, grammar schools, day schools and all manner of formal systems. Such systems take the child into a new, separate world, and their experience within formal education is artificial and systemically limited in nature. There is a narrow approach to learning, usually focused around the institution's structures, operating systems and ideology. The isolation of education systems – their segregation from the rest of society – enhances the feeling that learning in those systems has no clear relationship with the learning that children or society need.

The ways these systems operate have unintended impacts on their learners. A child who develops in an integrated social, emotional and intellectual environment at home faces a real contrast in school. Schools emphasize the intellectual at the expense of the social and emotional aspects of development. Most education institutions segregate children by their age, and judge them in isolation, not as social beings. This institutional method has emotional and educational consequences.

There may have been reasons for segregation by age, perhaps based on a starting point, when people arrived in the institutional setting. It may have developed from problems in schools that didn't separate children by age:

> I was only three when I first went to school. I went to school at such an early age because my mother was the schoolteacher and there weren't any babysitters. I remember the first day at school: I got spanked. That year I failed the first grade, so I had to do it again.
>
> (my father's memoir: a single-age school in Meno, Oklahoma, 1919)

This practice in turn led institutions to justify organizing learning in years. The belief is patently simplistic: children of the same age do not have the same academic or social abilities – their ages may be the same, but their needs are often different.

To keep children separate, regulated by age, exclusive of systematic contact with anyone else except an adult teacher, is not a normal way for people to learn. Individuals learn from others – older and younger others – and gain a sense of society by having society around them, impinging on their lives every day. Age-based classes, focused on a single adult (who is not part of the child's social group), can destroy a sense of normal society. Perhaps aspects of teenage culture arise because young people have to create social rules and behaviours because there are not the ordinary operations of all-age society around them. The control over teenagers exerted in schools is from an adult authority figure with, at times, draconian powers over the lives of others (and justified – if it is justified – solely by an educational function). With such an imbalanced social environment, it is not surprising that school culture is a distortion of the norms of society, rather than a model of good practice.

For many learners, having no familiar social structure in school is a disturbing contrast with their own home. Being judged as an individual is potentially threatening since this emphasizes isolation from caring others. The reasons for this emotionally barren approach in schools are largely historical, bureaucratic and economic. The unfortunate consequence is that positive emotional experiences are the exception in most education systems, and in the learning that occurs there.

The subject ghetto

Segregation in education even extends to what is taught. Historical models have knowledge separated into discrete areas of learning and these still dominate our approach to learning, though the subjects may have changed. Thus the Greeks and Romans studied rhetoric, whereas the closest modern equivalent is probably English, and eighteenth-century learners studied natural philosophy when today most of this area is called science. The approach has not changed: our educational world is divided into territories that become the focus of the system, its institutions, teachers, textbooks and examinations.

The fixation on subjects does distort the learning process, and at the moment has led to a tendency to emphasize a factual approach to learning. Some subjects can be quite different in different countries. History is a notorious example: Japanese children, for example, have only a limited grasp of Japanese war crimes in the Second World War, and English children have only a limited grasp of Russia's victory over Germany as a fundamental military story of the same war. In England, the Egyptians, Greeks and Romans are more important than Middle Eastern, Indian or Chinese civilizations. On the other hand, in Singapore, the Indian, South-east Asian and Chinese civilizations are important (and the word 'Japan' is rare).

The power of subjects and how they are structured into a programme for learning is actually quite important in determining learning in an education system. A subject-specific focus often creates learners that find it difficult to transfer their skills and knowledge from one country to another. Table 2.1 shows how the degrees from different countries vary in approach to subjects. The tension shown here is between eclectic, à la carte educational choice, (too) early specialization and a required core of subjects. None of the above operates an approach that is interdisciplinary, cutting across the subject boundaries. Within these systems you have choice, but not a choice of systems – so, for example, you cannot have a liberal arts degree if you do not happen to live in a country where universities offer them. One country's degrees are not always recognized by other countries: in Europe these problems have been so extreme that there has had to be a formal agreement between countries – the Bologna agreement – to recognize all European degrees (this came into force in 2007). Other qualifications have similar problems: dentists in Zürich are not yet free to act as dentists anywhere in Switzerland. The impact of the different

Table 2.1 Variations in approach to university degree subjects by country

Country	Preparation for university	University – first degree	Higher degrees
US and some others	Wide selection of courses, but within a subject framework that requires a range rather than a single focus	Liberal arts degrees, with a requirement to cover a range of subjects; 'major' and 'minor' emphasis	Almost all professional degrees, specialist degrees
England, Northern Ireland and others	Limited to three or four narrow subjects (A levels in French, music, physics or psychology, for example)	One subject only in most degrees; some professional degrees (law, education)	Within subject specialization, some professional conversion courses
Germany, parts of Japan (with variations)	Academic schools; technical schools; vocational schools	Academic; technical/industrial; vocation/business	Post-degree specialism within these areas

approach to subjects within universities has far-reaching effects: for example, historically students wishing to work in genetics often had to take a degree major in chemistry or biology, whereas now they can study biochemistry, biomedical sciences, genetic engineering or other degrees more tightly focused on the knowledge and skills they need.

Professional education has special features, one of which is the degree of control the profession has over accreditation – which often operates like the guild system in the Middle Ages. In the Middle Ages, a number of trades limited access to training, and therefore controlled the supply of skilled craftsmen (and women – if they were allowed to train in the craft at all). These restrictive practices have been copied by other professions through education systems. Medicine is an example of this. Although the demand for doctors and other workers in the health industry is very high, the access to training in some fields is artificially kept restricted. To become a doctor, initial entrance requirements for training (as in the UK and India) and/or the cost of training (as in the US) limit the number of doctors. This leads to the ridiculous situation of inflating the costs of medicine, with shortages in many areas. The incentive is that it increases the income of individual doctors and the medical profession generally. The contrast with the growth of the medical profession in the former Soviet Union, where the medical profession grew very rapidly to meet need, is instructive.

The experiences of students in different systems are often determined by the collection of subjects called the curriculum. These curricula restrict the learning experience of every child, and determine the time each child spends with a certain kind of learning experience. This can mean, for example, that all children in one country must study music to mid- or late secondary school, and only a few are allowed to do so in other countries.

Some countries (such as Singapore, Korea, the UK and Kenya) have a national curriculum, which includes a year-by-year detailed description of what should be taught. Other systems have local, state or regional arrangements and greater – or less – flexibility. In any case, a controlled presentation of learning by years and subjects increases uniformity, while making changes and adjustments very difficult. Resources, professional expertise and even the school buildings – once created to suit a curriculum – are hard to modify when new needs arise. Some schools – and governments – attempt creative recipes that enhance the basic ingredients: 'We currently offer the Kenya National Curriculum . . . it is flavoured with Computer Studies and French Language.'

Oddly enough, assigning time for procedural or skill-based learning is quite rare. Research into reading has implied that sustained silent reading (that is, for more than 20 minutes or so) is an important element in improving reading skills in secondary schools. Such time to read rarely appears in the curricular plans of schools.

None of this answers the question of what a 'subject' is. The nature of certain subjects' names, such as 'geography', illustrates the problems. Some would put geography as social science and others as science. Geography degrees are within environmental sciences at the University of South Africa, but within social sciences at the University of Chicago. Some subjects are actually united by a conceptual framework, as in the sciences, and can be 'science' in schools but then separate subjects at university. There are interrelationships that mean a single subject approach can distort. A classical example of this is literature, where ignoring the historical, intellectual, scientific and other-languages context of a work is not uncommon, but effectively prevents a full understanding of the text.

There are, however, more glaring issues. Educational systems tend not to acknowledge or give credit to certain kinds of learning. In some countries, such as Germany and England, vocational education attracts its own qualifications – separate but equal – but not official subject status. This separation of learning into acceptable and less acceptable, valid or less valid, is an institutional or system judgement, and varies from country to country, and from society to society.

The segregation of knowledge into subjects reveals tensions between education systems and society. Education systems are accused of being dominated by elitist people in ivory towers, interested only in creating more academics – rather than making a useful contribution to society. Subjects such as ancient Greek and Latin seem self-perpetuating irrelevances, when some areas in business, such as retail, struggle to gain a foothold. Equally, university education can be directed at research within the subject – specifically academic research – rather than real-life applications. There is a sense in which universities often lag behind changes in society, though society can often not respond to research. What is clear is that the interactions between the two sectors are often poor and this is a barrier to economic and social progress.

The demand for university courses in areas directly related to modern society is, however, very real. If subjects and curriculum are historically determined and slow to react to changes in employment, technology and society, learners remain keen on new developments in society. An obvious example is the response to the exponential growth in ICT, particularly the internet. When the Open University launched Technology 171 ('You, your computer, and the net') in the late 1990s, the course – developed by just six people – became one of the most popular ever established in a university anywhere in the world. This is matched by the huge growth in students of English in China through the China Central Radio and TV University.

Research findings in neuroscience conflict with the curriculum in certain countries, too. The problems here are well illustrated by the teaching of modern foreign languages. In the United Kingdom, teaching a modern foreign language was, until very recently, left until children were 11 or 12 years old. Most schools in the rest of Europe and Asia started teaching languages much earlier. There was clear evidence that leaving it until 11 was wrong:

> A group of researchers recently used MRI [magnetic resonance imaging] to obtain brain scans from children of ages 3 to 15 years. The researchers scanned the children's brains at intervals ranging from two weeks to four years, which allowed them to follow changes in their brains and construct 'growth maps' of the children's brain development . . . Thompson and colleagues found that the children's brains develop in a specific pattern, with a spurt of growth that starts in the front of the brain from ages 3 to 6. Between the ages 6 and 13, the researchers found that the pattern of rapid growth moves from the front to the back, toward the areas of the brain that are specialised for language skills. The researchers found that there is a sharp cut-off in the growth of the language areas of the brain after age 13. Another finding from the imaging study was that from age 13 to 15 about 50% of the brain tissue that controls motor skills are pruned away.
>
> (Blakemore: 16)

Other nations, probably correctly, had put language learning earlier – an interesting example of trial and error tending towards a solution that later gains scientific support. However, the English system had left it too late, condemning generations of adults to poor language skills – an example of the damage that education as an uncontrolled experiment can cause.

Subjects dominate education systems: resources, institutions, degrees and educators themselves all reflect a subject basis, and this focus on subjects – segregated areas of knowledge – can be as rigid as medieval education. Societies continue to change in response to economic and social development, and education limps behind, slow to change and committed to a set of subjects that often has only a historical pedigree – not an intellectual one.

Is school really like prison?

The comparison of schools to prisons is a commonplace (I found 70 million hits on Google alone) and, like popular comparisons generally, there is some truth behind it. Prisons, like schools, are a place to change behaviour through compulsion, routines and specially designed buildings. Whether or not life 'inside' is as bad in schools as in prisons is not really the point – the underlying similarities of approach are worrying. Learning is not spontaneous in education systems. There is daily compulsion in many ways, legal compulsion to attend school and economic compulsion to improve your life chances through qualifications. The economic pressure on parents to use schools as a child-minding facility is very real, too.

Often the core of the education system is a state enterprise, characterized by the state control of its staff, buildings and operation. Learners are physically segregated from society, from others of different ages (or religion or perceived ability), and their day-to-day existence is controlled by individuals with power in the institution (teachers). Often money is an issue and food is poor: indeed, about the same level of expenditure as on prison food is common. Society's declared purpose for these institutions might be described as creating valuable citizens and limiting social disruption: whatever it is, the children are rarely consulted.

The routines in education are restrictive: what is taught is tightly controlled through the curriculum; when it is taught is tightly controlled by daily timetables; where it is taught – even within the building – is determined; and education's purposes are externally imposed. The feel of education in school can be repressive, and people within education can be desensitized by the system. This is true of teachers, even though most are committed to learning and fond of children. At times education systems can become brutal and even criminal. Togo has recently been a focus for criticism, with beatings and abusive behaviour apparently common, but few societies can claim to have an education system without scandals. Japan has had to change its approach to children's emotional well-being in part because of the extreme behaviour of some schools and teachers. In almost any society, the invitation 'Let me teach you a lesson' can be threatening and, like bad parents, there are bad teachers. Yet most teachers, despite the pressures and bureaucratic burden, continue to struggle to make things work for young people.

Education buildings reflect education systems. Learning spaces are rect-angular boxes for groups of 30, with some special areas, such as a space to talk to (or at) large groups. Most learners in school and university face an endless sequence of rectilinear spaces in drab colours and cheap furniture. Curiously education buildings can be quite expensive to build because of the educa-tional industry's very rigid 'requirements'. An education building is easy to recognize, even though the essential ideas are derived from different buildings altogether. The most basic approach has been 'school as house' (see Figure 2.1), where the architecture, size and materials were essentially the same as conventional houses. This embodies the role of the school as an extension of the family, where children are brought together with a surrogate parent (the teacher), paid for by the community, to teach them what is considered by the community as important. Such schools tend to be within walking distance of local homes.

Another common approach is 'school as church/temple', embodying a dominant belief system in the region (see Figure 2.2). The school as church has always been popular in residential institutions – whether schools or universities – where the physical distance from home indicates the relative

Figure 2.1 'School as house': Nicodemus, Kansas, 1915

Source: Library of Congress, *American Memory* archive (http://memory.loc.gov/ammem/index.html)

Figure 2.2 'School as church': Fairfield, Utah, 1898

Source: Library of Congress, *American Memory* archive (http://memory.loc.gov/ammem/index.html)

wealth of the parents and a desire for some degree of exclusiveness. The building serves as a physical reminder of the ideological focus of the institution and the learning within it.

In modern, urban areas the 'school as factory' (see Figure 2.3) has become popular with educationalists, especially for the later stages of education (though in Hiroshima and other areas in Japan very large primary schools on this model exist). The idea that education systems use a factory model, with the mass production of ordinary working children, is strengthened by the appearance of such buildings. Education buildings of this kind probably reflect the constraints of urban sites and architectural styles in industry. The effect is to emphasize the economic functions of learning.

There are, of course, many variations of these themes. Newly built schools have not made radical changes in layout and function, but have tended to perpetuate schools with classrooms, rectangular spaces where children can listen to the teacher, and where education is not so different from what it was a hundred years ago.

Is there any escape?

The all-pervasive nature of education systems in modern life make escape from the system difficult. In theory there are ways of opting out through home

Figure 2.3 'School as factory': Monaco, Pennsylvania, 1933
Source: Library of Congress, *American Memory* archive (http://memory.loc.gov/ammem/index.html)

schooling, but in practice these are ways to control how a child interacts with the education system. The system dictates the qualifications accepted by most employers, the system dictates the subjects, and the system controls societal expectations of individuals. Parents educating their children is a means to unite home and school experiences under one roof. Parents do not, however, know how to support a child's learning with any more certainty than individual teachers in the education system, and are just as likely to make mistakes. Often children taught at home simply use the same methods and resources as are used in schools. There are differences. Advocates of home schooling claim improved progress of children or a firmer acceptance of the family's religion or world view. Parents who choose these options are not necessarily comparing like with like, since they rarely consider what would happen if the money they spent on home education (including the parents' time) was spent instead on supplementing free education.

There are no easy answers to how we can ensure people learn, but there are methods to find better answers. Current education systems are not the only viable options, or even adequate ones. Nor are education systems fixed forever, and segregation and compartmentalization in learning are not inevitable. It is possible to create better ways to learn.

Chapter 3

Globalizing learning

壮游　　　From **Travels in my Prime**

七龄思即壮　I was already bright at seven
开口咏风凰　When I wrote my first poem – *The Phoenix*.
九龄书大字　By nine I loved composing. Teenaged:
有作成一囊　Unconventional, I liked drinking;
性豪业嗜酒　Strong-minded, I hated corruption.
嫉恶怀刚肠　I abandoned thoughts of a child
脱落小时辈　and searched for the wise.
结交皆老苍　We'd get drunk: talking together
饮酣视八极　I'd grasp the whole universe
俗物多茫茫　All at once, cutting free
　　　　　　From the commonplace.

Du Fu (721–770 CE) also known as Tu Fu,
considered the world's greatest poet

A biological reality check

There are no biological differences in learning capacity between peoples – regardless of outward appearance, religion or nationality. From a biological perspective, what at times keeps people apart – such as differences in culture or behaviour – does not reflect any underlying difference at all. It has taken people centuries to accept this and, indeed, there are some people who have not accepted it yet. The conflicts between cultures, religions, ideologies and nations are not based on biological differences but on learned behaviour. All peoples have a similar capacity to learn. While most accept the principle of equal worth, it is not accepted in our schools and universities.

The biological reality that human capacity to learn is universal – not specific to groups – should have sparked a search for the kinds of learning that humans are disposed towards. The differences in subjects in different education systems perhaps obscured the common set of learning outcomes for all people. Equally, the separation of education from some learned behaviours – such as skills related to interacting with other people (despite their centrality in human life and society) – may have masked obvious global givens. The growth of psychology has helped, though psychology has a tendency to avoid formal education (particularly the teaching of psychology). The brain's common biological blueprint suggests there is no justification in the segregation of learners by religion, nationality or many of the other ways in which learning is currently compartmentalized. The endless variety of education systems probably inhibits improvements in learning by isolating educationalists and obscuring evidence of successful practice. Or, to put it more simply, because it is often accepted that education is specific to each country (or religion, or group), we fail to work together to improve learning for everyone: there is no agreement, for example, on how to teach religion in Northern Ireland.

The differences between education systems are often based on the assumption that nationality, religion, culture and language require fundamental differences in children's educational experiences. This argument has no scientific basis at all (that is to say, there is no sound evidence that different nationalities, religions or linguistic groups have different genetic, biological or neurological differences). There is no sensible non-political argument for national education systems (that is, arguments not based on some form of political agenda). This is also the case with religious education systems. The function of such systems is to encourage belief in a religion. The importance of education as a means of maintaining a faith is self-evident, but this is an incentive for religious institutions, not for the child. There is no natural right of a nation, religion or ideology to inculcate a world view in children – yet it is common practice.

Language is a different matter. Children generally understand what they are taught more easily in their own language, and there are areas in the world where some degree of multilingualism is normal (such as Luxembourg, Switzerland and Belgium). Languages do not, however, require a radically different education or specific world view. Thoughts are not determined by our language, though they may be coloured by it, as Pinker has eloquently shown:

> But it is wrong, all wrong. The idea that thought is the same thing as language is an example of what can be called a conventional absurdity ... Think about it. We have all had the experience of uttering or writing a sentence, then stopping and realizing that it wasn't what we meant to say. To have that feeling, there has to be a 'what we meant to say' that is different from what we said.
>
> (Pinker: 37)

The independence of thought from language does not change the practical advantages of teaching in the child's native language. On the other hand, language does not determine what should be taught, or how it is to be understood.

The localization of education can even be to units smaller than nation states, religious or linguistic groups, as in Germany and the United States. From Northern Ireland to Israel and Palestine, from Brazil's Indian languages to the Portuguese of Rio, education is currently used to continue the differences that divide the world. The idea that it is necessary to have local control over education presupposes that there is a distinct local element in learning. Realistically, this is hardly likely to be possible, never mind true: a biological reality unites all people – the human brain.

There are encouraging signs of a more cooperative approach between education systems. The European Union has brought many different nations together in a region historically bedevilled by war and sectarianism. Although education systems are not supposed to be a focus of the European Union, this is actually far from the case. European projects on learning and many projects in other areas require people to work across education systems: there is a European SchoolNet for international cooperation, and Europe has funded a range of educational initiatives looking at ways to increase common educational development. One such development is in languages, where there is now an international system of accreditation in modern languages, used in all countries: the European Languages Portfolio. There are pilot European schools with a common educational approach, an ICT programme and qualification (the European Computer Driving Licence) and other educational initiatives. The globalizing of learning has started in other areas as well, and through other organizations such as the United Nations (UN) and the OECD international educational cooperation is growing. These changes have parallels in industry: there are more international standards where there are globalized industries, but the trend towards globalized standards is strong. Learning organizations have begun to become international: from the Open University's presence in most of the countries on earth to the ambitious programme of MIT (Massachusetts Institute of Technology) to share its courses freely through the internet, there is an active expansion in the university sector into other countries.

This globalization is not confined to organizations: people around the world are increasingly able to access learning wherever they are. China's attempts to limit the impact of the internet on its populace are an object lesson: it may be possible to control the flow of information and knowledge to some extent, but in the end the internet is irrevocably globalizing information. In this kind of world, people and organizations can help each other improve learning, starting with learning from their educational differences.

Learning from our differences

While it is difficult for economists to perform experiments . . . the world provides a vast array of natural experiments as dozens of countries try different strategies. Unfortunately, because each country differs in . . . the myriad of details in the policies . . . it is often difficult to get a clear

Figure 3.1 Internet access without political censorship: it will be there soon
Source: courtesy of www.freedigitalphotos.net

interpretation. What is clear, however, is that there have been marked
differences in performance . . . the most successful countries have been
those in Asia.

(Stiglitz: 29)

Differences between education systems will prove to be extremely useful in
the short term. The ability to compare systems – and how successful children
are within those systems – is a natural experiment that can indicate what
approaches to learning are effective. For example, a number of studies have
examined the success of minorities in education systems. The interesting
outcome of these studies is that, for a child, being in a minority is likely to
inhibit learning slightly – so, for example, members of a particular group
will do well where they are in the majority, but less well when they are in
a small minority. An example of this is the white children in Hong Kong
– a small minority – who do less well than the white children in the UK – a
large majority – even when other factors are kept constant. It suggests
relatively poor educational outcomes for minority groups depend not on
culture, ethnicity or social group but on whether members of the group are in
the minority within each educational setting.

Fundamental questions about education systems can also be explored through large international studies. The OECD, the European Union and the UN are the leading organizations that carry out this kind of research. One classic question to ask about education systems is: if more money is spent on education, do children do better? Most people's instinctive response is to think that money matters a lot, but the OECD PISA studies show it is not so straightforward. To begin with, comparing educational outcomes is not easy, as children study different subjects in different ways. Equally, determining the real value of expenditure on education is not simple: teachers in poorer countries cost less to employ, for example. Leaving aside all these complications, the picture that emerges from these studies is quite revealing, as Figure 3.2 shows.

The left-hand scale indicates the average performance in reading, using measurements created to be fair across the many countries. The scale at the bottom shows the number of US dollars spent per child in terms of purchasing power. The first striking feature is how educational outcomes seem to bunch between 480 and 520 on the reading score regardless of expenditure. This bunching of results suggests that there might be a core level of reading competency that most countries reach, but few exceed. The second is that some countries (e.g. Austria) spend almost eight times as much per child as others (e.g. Mexico), yet their education systems are still less successful than those that cost less in other countries.

The diagonal line is the average trend, which suggests that more money tends to lead to better results – but not hugely better ones. There are distinctive differences too: the performance of Finland is a sharp contrast to that of

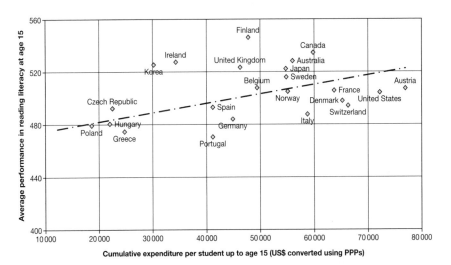

Figure 3.2 Student performance and spending per student

Source: OECD 2000

Portugal though their expenditure is about equal. An uncomfortable conclusion might be that in education governments do not know what to spend extra money on in order to make outcomes better.

Many of the studies carried out by the OECD, European Union and UN concentrate on education as a key factor in economic growth and development. In doing this, there are questions of social equity – for example, does extra spending on education benefit the poor – or the rich? Does education make society more or less equal? Again, the outcomes from such studies indicate that there are no straightforward answers – see Figure 3.3.

The left-hand scale indicates the average outcome for children's literacy (higher up the scale being better). The scale along the bottom indicates how much impact family background has on individual children's achievement – broadly speaking, educationally successful families have educationally successful children. The OECD was looking to see if a system might be increasing achievement at the same time as reducing inequality.

Again, the comparisons are interesting. Every system seemed to give an advantage to those who were already advantaged, but in Japan and Korea that difference was smallest. It is tempting to think that the systems in Germany and Luxembourg were not as good because Germany seemed to have a substantial social gap and Luxembourg pupils did not do well. There may be other causes: the unification of Germany and the linguistic demands on Luxembourg's children. However, there is little doubt that education systems are not all equally effective, or equally fair to the disadvantaged. There appears

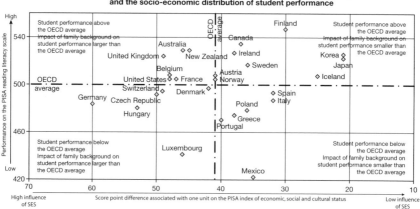

Note: The mean reading performance in five countries is not statistically different from the OECD average: Denmark, France, Norway, Switzerland and the United States. The socio-economic distribution of student performance in eight countries is not statistically different from the OECD average: Austria, Denmark, Greece, Ireland, New Zealand, Norway, Poland and Portugal.
For the definition of the PISA index of economic, social and cultural status, see Annex 1, 'Knowledge and Skills for Life', PISA 2000.

Figure 3.3 Relationship between PISA reading literacy and socio-economic distribution of student performance

Source: OECD 2000

to be evidence in this research that children do better where all schools are similar (Finland) and where all children are taught a demanding curriculum (Japan and Korea), and that the education systems of successful economies are also better. 'The average level of education in South Korea in 1960 was less than four years; today, South Korea leads in high-tech industries such as chip production, and its income has increased sixteenfold in the past forty years' (Stiglitz: 31).

There is an economic incentive that drives such interest in education in the OECD countries: the belief that better educational outcomes have a positive impact on the economy. Analysis of the growth of nations by the OECD, the European Union and the UN all demonstrate this, particularly in the early stages of economic development. There are certain aspects of education that seem more important than others: the pivotal role of science and technology, its impact on improving security in the world and the overall impact of simple access to education as a driving force of development. Arguments of this kind support heavy investment in core education in science and technology across countries as a way to increase economic growth and prosperity. However, educational development continues to be contained within the national or even regional governments in Europe, North America and the OECD countries. One reason for this might be politicians' belief that countries prosper by competing, even in education. This belief appears to be ill-founded, as the cooperation of countries in East Asia has shown: countries agreed to have complementary specialisms in economic growth areas using new technologies, and work together to provide a cohesive technological infrastructure. Their reward was the best economic growth of any set of countries.

From the learners' point of view, any education that does not help prepare them for a global future ignores their economic interests. A young person has more economic choices if they are familiar with other countries, if they are educated to a high standard that is recognized in more economies, and if they are not pressured to stay in one place geographically, politically or socially. In other words, for the young it is a globalized future, and they may feel they do not belong to the society that raises them. Economic theory would suggest they are right: by not being bound to a specific country, place or religion the flow of human capital will more easily follow need, and the world economy will prosper more rapidly – and so will they. In moral terms the argument might be that education should help the young to learn in a way that maximizes their economic potential, rather than artificially restricting them to living in the society that educated them.

Incentives are clearly there for young people and their parents for globalized learning linked to economic globalization. Few would argue with the principle of all people on earth having access to opportunities to learn, or with the premise that everyone should have opportunities to access those aspects of learning that are most likely to benefit them in later life. These beliefs are integral to most societies' values, though sometimes only implicitly. The compartmentalization of education we allow in so many different ways offers a useful natural experiment, but it is, in the end, something that inhibits educational improvement and the economic opportunities of individuals, families and societies.

Learning as neuroscience

A truly international approach to learning already exists in neuroscience and related sciences. This approach concentrates on the brain's biochemistry and structure as a single organ where adaptation to the environment – or learning – occurs. The research to date has made many begin to see what and how people learn in terms of neuroscientific processes. Since within the brain biological mechanisms for learning and cognition are largely inbuilt, the development of these areas – learning in general – is also common across appearance, religion and nationality.

Neuroscientific research has given immediate indications that education systems could improve. For example, it appears broadly true that successful learning is primarily a question of time spent in learning (for example, in music or sport). This makes the usual division of children into those that are good learners and those that are bad learners illogical. Even worse is reducing the amount and nature of learning practice for the weakest. This is exactly contrary to the biological logic (where more time means more improvement). It would be like having the least physically fit students do the least exercise (actually, this tends to happen in education, too) – when they self-evidently need to do more. Another interesting consideration is that the weakest would gain strength more quickly than the strong – that is, they would gain a greater proportional benefit per hour of exercise. There is an immediate way of improving things: give more time to those that need it most.

How people learn in education systems is dominated by a very restricted approach from a neurological perspective: literally a medieval approach to learning, emphasizing the exposition of knowledge as a set of facts, subjects and formal rules – knowledge that should be remembered and declared. This kind of learning, with declarative memory at its heart, is the basis of what is taught: it is easier to measure but arguably less important than other ways humans learn. For example, procedural memory (loosely speaking, 'skills') is often neglected. Such skills are sometimes difficult to state as facts or to assess with a grade or mark, but that does not stop them being extremely powerful learning mechanisms. Most people can do things flawlessly without necessarily knowing the declarative basis that makes them possible:

> Take cycling as an example . . . what about cornering? What is the first thing to do when you want to turn left, for example? You might think 'turn the handlebars to the left', but you would be wrong. By slowing down films of people cycling, it became possible to see that they first turned briefly in the 'wrong' direction: in our example, to the right. This

causes the bicycle to start falling to the left. It is necessary to lean to the left when turning left, so this partial fall has to precede the actual turn.

(Open University course SD226: Unit 5: 10)

Many skills, such as playing musical instruments, are not dependent on explicitly linking huge numbers of facts; to a neuroscientist, they are procedural, not declarative, functions. The balance between procedural memory and declarative memory – between being able to state and being able to do – has been cited frequently as a weakness in formal education systems. This is actually because they have different physical origins in the processes of the brain:

> It is well known that [certain] amnesic patients . . . have severely impaired declarative memory – they are unable to learn and retain new facts. However, they are able to learn new skills and they retain skills they acquired before their brain damage. For example, a severely amnesic patient who used to be a pianist has no memory for events that happened more than five minutes earlier, but is nonetheless able to play the piano as perfectly as he could before . . . patients are also able to acquire new skills, despite not explicitly remembering being taught the skill. . . . [On the other hand] Patients with Parkinson's disease . . . have good memory for episodes and facts, but they are unable to learn new skills. In other words, there seems to be a dissociation between declarative and procedural learning, confirmed by recent functional imaging studies . . . For purposes of teaching it might be important to know that learning facts, such as mathematical equations and historical dates, relies on different brain regions than learning to do sport or play a musical instrument. A possible research question is whether the two kinds of learning can occur in parallel rather than each . . . be taught separately.
>
> (Blakemore: 23)

The distinction is not between physical and mental activity but between different processes of learning. At one end of the continuum of learning people are able to learn without being taught at all: they can learn complex sequences and the underlying patterns and use them, without consciously being aware, which is termed implicit learning. Implicit learning can be directly demonstrated in experiments:

> People can learn complex rules by being exposed to sequences that adhere to the rules, without having any explicit notion of the rules or having learned them . . . Subjects performed a simple reaction-time task in which all stimuli were equally likely but, unknown to them, they actually followed a complex sequence. Subjects' behavioural performance indicated that they learned the sequences even though they were unaware of the existence of any order . . . suggests that the ventral striatum is responsive

to novel information, and the right prefrontal area is associated with the maintenance of contextual information, and both processes can occur without awareness.

(Blakemore: 22)

The brain's ability to deal with constant environmental input shows a wide range of responses. As cognition becomes more complicated different areas of the brain, and different processes in the brain, come into play. People learn constantly without being taught or even being motivated to learn. Imagine a young boy going shopping with his family: there will be latent learning (wandering around a shopping mall holding his mother's hand he will learn its layout), observational learning (seeing his father push a button to bring down a lift gives him knowledge of how to do it) and one-trial learning (smoothies are nice). All this indicates that declarative memory – the mainstay of much education – is only a small part of learning. It may also suggest why subjects and declarative teaching can inhibit learners' ability to transfer understanding between areas of knowledge (a common problem in education systems).

The way people learn is more varied than formal education takes account of in schools and universities. Neuroscientific research indicates there are tremendous opportunities to improve by concentrating on a wider variety of methods (such as games approaches) and using latent, procedural and other processes. The simple message is that better learning is possible, and discovering how offers a clear rationale for working together globally.

Learning is social

New knowledge in neuroscience can challenge the fundamental assumptions of many educators, and also help unify our concept of learning. Another way to look at this process is to consider how learning operates in homes and socially, and what this might contribute to understanding learning in other contexts. For example, good parenting seeks to be positive, solution-orientated and emotionally supportive. In such environments, learning tends to be more intuitive, emotionally sound and naturally occurring. There is little emphasis on overt control as good parents use incentives – positive emotional feedback, rewards, thoughtfulness – and they model learning by learning themselves. The key outcome is to help their child become well adapted to the whole of their environment, and to enjoy learning. This contrasts with the formality, individual isolation and routines of many education systems. Not surprisingly in education systems the motivated learner is an ideal, and there is a growing realization that an integrated vision of the whole person offers a better understanding of how to achieve this:

Motivation is not a single entity . . . Learning, too, is a complex phenomenon that cannot be conceived as a single entity . . . The American

Psychological Association's 'Learner Centered Psychological Principles' include cognitive and metacognitive factors, motivational and affective factors, developmental and social factors, and individual difference factors.

(EPPI, Harlen *et al*.: 1–2)

The rather clinical language of psychological and neuroscientific research of this kind obscures the central message that the whole person – their feelings, thoughts, intuitions, self concept, social roles and so on – are central to their learning. That all these factors are located in the brain – a single, physical organ – shows that the whole person is actually one 'thing' and society's mental and physical segregation of learning into formal and informal sectors is largely artificial. Developing motivation – a disposition and will to actively learn – is partly achieved through opportunities to learn and to develop different kinds of learning skills. It is probable that learning is easiest as a fundamental process within families and wider social groups as a collaborative, dynamic process, since so many motivational factors in humans are social and emotional.

Historically emotion has been seen by many educators to be distinct from and at odds with other forms of cognition and with the purposes of education. In neuroscience emotions are now seen as an integral part of human thought, based on the same neurological mechanisms as other forms of cognition. Or, more directly, social, emotional and intellectual thought are artificial divisions in what is really an integrated process: the biochemical operations of the human brain and body. The change in perspective is similar to rejecting the distinction between mind and body (or brain and mind). Leading neuroscientists have modelled emotion as consistent with other forms of cognition and suggested how it interacts with other forms of cognition: 'one of the key purposes of our educational development is to interpose a nonautomatic evaluative step between causative objects and emotional responses.'

Emotion is key to people's ability to make sophisticated judgements in a fraction of a second – the theme of Gladwell's best-selling book, *Blink*. Such judgements are taken through emotional responses, and can be seen as a fundamental part of the intellectual process:

> it is useful to think of emotional reactions as an inference or best guess providing a rough and ready shortcut for creating prompt action. Even the cleverest of us, provided with unlimited library and computer facilities, would be unable to have access to all the information *in time* to make a rational decision in most situations that give rise to emotions . . . emotions, or their equivalent, are essential for any intelligent being . . . If an intelligent system has a number of different motivations or goals, then something like emotions would be required to set priorities among them, and to allow events to interrupt what the . . . individual was doing.
>
> (OU SD226: Unit 6, 73)

This is an important argument: seeing emotion as a rapid response to complex situations, and preparing for further analysis means emotion is a vital process that can link a variety of responses and can be made more sophisticated. Nor are emotional or unconscious aspects of cognition somehow the opposite of consciously ethical behaviours. Damasio, a leading neuroscientist, has argued 'Ethical behaviors are a subset of social behaviors', a conclusion built upon the research into ethical behaviours in animals and humans. Learning is an adaptive response to the environment, and the evolutionary function of ethical behaviour is clear: 'any genetic contribution toward cooperative behaviour would be favoured by natural selection. It is believed that this social cooperation has been an important factor in the development of human ethics.'

Neuroscientists go further by identifying that 'the biological mechanisms underlying ethical behaviour' are essentially emotional in origin but become linked to other processes in the brain in similar ways to higher-order mechanisms in many other forms of cognition: 'the systems that support ethical behaviors are probably not dedicated to ethics exclusively. They are dedicated to biological regulation, memory, decision-making, and creativity. Ethical behaviors are the wonderful and most useful side effects of those other activities.' This implies the fundamental importance of emotional and social cognition in learning as well as in life as a whole.

Equally, the whole environment impacts on learning whether it is home, work, formal education, economic or technological. People tend to see homes and formal education as where learning occurs. Employers often do little to support learning except through the job routines and training that is often formal, impersonal and not enjoyable. Employees, however, can often build strong social networks within employment, and this can have a significant impact on the success of the business. A holistic, neuroscientific assessment sees learning in every environment and, broadly speaking, as a dominantly social process. A proof of this is the many methods people have created to communicate: language, writing, telephones, the mass media, the internet and many others. Knowledge itself is socially constructed, as is its transfer between people. As the power of society to communicate grows, the richness of the human social environment grows: for some, there is instant access to others through mobile phones, the ability to share anything digital across the world in seconds through the internet and the growing flexibility in when and where they work. These trends are towards more flexibility in learning and living, with fewer barriers between people: globalizing learning, a process that may, in the end, bring people closer together.

Globalizing learning

Globalizing learning is a process in which there are a number of themes, largely to do with a focus on individual learners rather than systems or bureaucracies. It is easy to forget how long people have tried to systematize learning through bureaucracy as part of globalization-type strategies. The best example is probably China. Faced with uniting what was the world's largest country, the Chinese established a civil service structure that has helped secure its survival as the longest continuous civilization. This success is impressive, and it has been imitated, consciously or not, by the British and other empires. As an early attempt at a form of globalization it had real strengths, as did the single written language. Education for roles in the civil service became formalized into a rigid structure, and much like the training for Egypt's priesthood or the Roman army, this structure ossified and became a barrier to improvement. The Chinese also developed an examination system for entry to governmental positions and thus created one of the world's most enduring culturally specific literary themes (as the impact of examination failure on people's lives is a distinctively Chinese *motif*). The examinations were largely literary, based on classical texts and formal commentaries and, not sur- prisingly, produced a lot of skilled literary critics but not good government (poets fared less well – Du Fu failed when a royal whim caused all candidates to fail). Though the aim of the system was laudable – the equal promotion of talent and skills in government – the method was not good enough, and the consequences unfortunate in that Chinese bureaucracy became very corrupt and inefficient. This kind of examination-based learning tragedy has been used in many countries for billions of people with similar results. With hindsight, the declared purpose of the Chinese to seek talent wherever it could be found was astute, but the means were not: there may be better solutions at some point in the future.

Looked at from a learner's point of view (rather than a system view) globalization starts with unifying the worlds of home, education and work. This is not just a question of television and the internet creating a global village but also a question of looking at other issues such as social and emotional needs in all environments. For example, it is often asserted that activities in education have no real-life purpose contributing to the well-being of others, as activities usually do in homes, work and leisure. Education routines can be unnecessarily rigid. The individual's procedural, implicit and other forms of learning are used more often in homes, whereas declarative memory is dominant in education. In work it depends on the context, but there is usually relatively little stress on declarative learning. All of this implies imbalances in the use of learning strategies that need addressing in all three environments.

Measuring progress can be important for learners – from riding bicycles to reading. If measurements of learning across all learners are needed within society, the methods of modern social science are a positive alternative to formal examinations for all. This alternative approach to most assessment focuses on the needs of the learner, not the system. Assessment can be used to support the individual learner, helping to identify what they have already mastered and what the next steps should be. It can also identify an individual's potential or social skills. International assessments, though used to support the learner, can be used to measure their progress to date and their potential in comparison with other learners and across different societies. Measuring the effectiveness of the education system itself can also be achieved using the sampling techniques of modern social science. For example, to check on the progress of a country's 16 year olds it would be necessary to sample the progress of only about 20,000 students. This approach to assessment is better for learners, cheaper and more accurate than testing every child in the nation. Changes in measurement such as this follow exactly the same processes the sciences followed when adopting the metric system: they created common measurements, and through this speeded the transfer of scientific and technological information between countries.

In an increasingly globalized world, it is even more important to encourage children to learn about different world views, political systems, languages and cultures. Most schools and universities in the United States, France, Turkey and other secular societies are not religious, but only a tiny minority of them strive to be international politically. Holland is one of the few countries that has an education system that is strongly biased towards an international world view. There are pragmatic reasons for education free from indoctrination, in that it allows different individuals, institutions, groups, societies and countries to work together to improve learning. This happens with some university-level resources, particularly the sciences. On a larger scale, it offers scope for international cooperation and the development of human resources that are of mutual benefit.

These kinds of changes in education move it away from idiosyncratic systems towards a universal process. Such a movement is a small part of creating an educational environment where we can start to seek improvements in learning in the same way we seek improvements in medicine – in a world-wide, cooperative context. Like medicine, it may well mean tensions between commercial and public sectors, failures of the process through mistakes, and increasing costs and complexity. Like medicine, huge advances are not just possible but are achievable in relatively short timescales – at least in comparison with the longevity of the classical Chinese examination system.

Building for learning

The physical environment in schools, universities and classrooms has been the subject of interesting speculation and visionary ideas, but generally remains very largely conservative in approach. In the US there has been a major reconsideration of school buildings and a large building programme leading to some modifications, most notably towards smaller high schools. In New Zealand, Holland, Australia, Japan, Norway and other countries there have been some very bold experiments in learning environments. New Zealand's

National School for Science and Technology has no classrooms at all, with a large, open space for all learning activities. There have also been experimental approaches to the methods of learning in education, for example in Montessori schools. Neither the changes in the buildings nor the changes in the methods of learning have been based on rigorous research into learning, and so – while interesting – such innovations are unlikely to have a significant long-term impact.

The faults of educational buildings are to some extent universal. This is evident when children are asked what they want school buildings to be like, as they all appear to have similar priorities. The Sorrell Foundation, a UK charity that links famous designers with schoolchildren, found thousands of children in over 60 schools came up with a remarkably similar set of concerns – see 'What children want' (p. 54).

The qualities these children sought are an interesting reflection of their priorities. One set centred on qualities of homes: a sense of colour; social eating, talking and relaxing; personal space for socializing and work; hygienic toilets; and a strong social emphasis on welcoming others well. Other priorities are: good communication; understanding the communal purpose ('inspiring', 'proud' and 'vision'). There is almost nothing about ideal learning itself – no requests for comfortable seating, computers, swimming pools or libraries – perhaps a reflection of the assumption that active learning spaces are outside their control. The overall emphasis strongly suggests that, for children, as well as social concerns, a feeling of emotional well-being is central. There are parallels with what many might consider a good adult working environment here.

One of the outcomes of building programmes in the US has been some research into the relationship between buildings and learning. A good US overview of the research commented: 'But which facility attributes affect academic outcomes the most and in what manner and degree? A growing body of research addresses these questions. Some of it is good, some less so; much of it is inconclusive.' The key findings discussed in the research review identified the physical aspects (air, light and sound) as more likely to have a direct positive impact on health and achievement than the building age and quality. The best learning environments were, in effect, the best working environments for people generally: good natural light, fresh air, good acoustics and a well-presented and well-maintained building. As in work or homes, good learning flourishes in good, healthy environments. Other large national building programmes have considered size of schools and, perhaps, classes. This building research was not linked to rigorous research into the curriculum, teaching methods and outcomes – and the concern with learning has not played any significant part in such programmes. The focus was often simply on recreating the education of the past in a better building.

The process used in the creation of these building programmes varies between countries. For example, the UK national building programme came

What children want

COLOUR
They want to brighten up their schools and use colour to enhance atmosphere and mood.

COMMUNICATION
They want to tell pupils, teachers, parents and the community what is going on.

DINNER HALLS AND CANTEENS
They want a civilized lunch time with less chaos and more time to relax.

LEARNING SPACES
They want inspiring places to learn.

RECEPTION AREAS
They want parents, new pupils, the local community and visitors to feel welcome.

REPUTATION AND IDENTITY
They want to be proud of their school and be sure what it stands for.

SIXTH-FORM SPACES
They want rooms where they can socialize and work on their own.

SOCIAL SPACES
They want sheltered spaces to 'chat and chill' during breaks.

STORAGE
They want secure places to put their books, stationery, equipment, bags and coats.

TOILETS
They want toilets to be clean, hygienic and safe.

UNIFORM
They want comfortable, smart, 'cool looking' clothes that they will be proud to wear.

WHOLE SCHOOL PLAN
They want to contribute to a vision for a new school.

JoinedUpDesignForSchools, The Sorrell Foundation, UK

after the US programme: discussions were held with the Education Minister, then David Miliband, about ensuring the cost effectiveness of this large public sector investment. One outcome was not to build schools one at a time, on a case-by-case basis, as it had been for many years, but to build them simultaneously, updating all the schools in a whole area at the same time. This meant that contractors could bid to build a number of schools simultaneously within a fairly small area. The actual design of the buildings was a lower priority but recognized as an important aspect of developing a learning environment that reflected the twenty-first century rather than the nineteenth. Mukund Patel, of the UK's Department for Education and Skills (DfES), was responsible for design issues and had already created a series of small-scale pilot projects looking at classrooms of the future, workspaces for the staff of the future and, finally, Building Schools for the Future (the national building programme's ambitious title). A series of innovatory designs, called 'Exemplar Designs', were created to encourage innovation and create free templates that would allow companies to benefit from economies of scale by using the same template for many schools.

Despite this encouragement to innovate, the implementation of the UK's school building programme to date has been beset with a worryingly conservative response from educationalists and construction contractors. Many of the schools have been built as a modern version of existing school designs, complete with rectangular classrooms. 'Innovation' has often been limited to having electronic whiteboards rather than blackboards, and the basic model has remained firmly conventional. The reasons for this conservatism include the rigid control the DfES still insisted on in terms of the curriculum, the size and number of classrooms, the other spaces in the building and the financial restraints. The incentives to stay the same were powerful: greater profits through re-using existing designs and approaches, and dealing with a risk-averse client group. Forces such as these tend to keep all educational buildings conventional in most countries. There were, however, some attempts to innovate through creating flexible spaces that could evolve with the changes in learning.

Learning villages

Figure 3.4 The learning village

Source: courtesy of de Rijke Marsh Morgan architects

The innovation in school buildings that was fostered by Mukund Patel's pilot projects and exemplar school designs is worth examining briefly. The designs indicate the willingness to consider a more radical approach to school buildings, an opportunity taken up by de Rijke Marsh Morgan (dRMM) architects. The initial concept was a learning village in a protective environment, and one that is able to include other organizations in its dome – a mini-city, if you like (see Figure 3.4). The final design was called the Dura (the membrane that encloses the brain). It was engineered to have very low environmental impact, and the architects also tried to address the issues raised by the research into what features in a building improve learning.

The domed roof is ETFE (Ethylene/Tetrafluoroethylene), a transparent plastic film, making a climatic barrier. One immediate consequence is excellent transmission of natural light – one of the key features of a desirable working environment. The second feature is acoustical transparency – the noise goes out of the building rather than bouncing back in. A third feature is that the space is protected from the environment, so all enclosed spaces inside (rooms) can be constructed in wood (off site) and reconfigured as required. The approach to indoor air quality, thermal performance and energy use is strikingly simple, using modern sustainability techniques. The particular concepts are often simple, albeit technically ingenious: one is the use of an earth tube that sucks in air from the outside through an underground channel that allows it to be naturally warmed to the ambient temperature

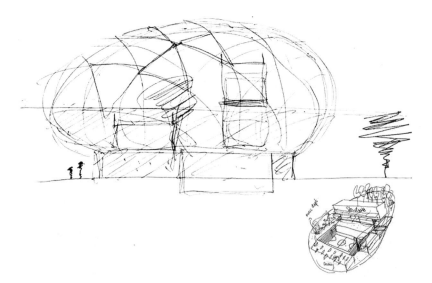

Figure 3.5 The learning village: initial sketch

Source: courtesy of de Rijke Marsh Morgan architects

under the ground (about 12°C in England). The temperature of the people inside the building also increases the temperature within the building, and so a pleasant climate is created. Another important aspect is that the air is drawn through the building naturally, without mechanical air pumps. It all seems simple, and these techniques are already in use in many buildings.

One of the features of the dRMM design is a commitment to a consciously radical approach to the architecture of learning, a building that is both rational (supported by good evidence), and reconfigurable (able to respond to changes in needs). There were conflicts between this approach and the innate conservatism of elements within the DfES intent on keeping control over the curriculum, its delivery and the nature of spaces in educational buildings. As an example, the Dura appeared to give more internal space than the regulations specified, but within the same total cost. A major argument arose that, in the end, was won by the design team supported by the more progressive elements within the DfES.

The ETFE roof allows the school to have open spaces and classrooms of any shape. The shape dRMM used as the fundamental one for groups to work in was a triangle, partly because of the benefits of the shape – as it tessellates – but also because it is cheaper to create a shape that minimizes the length of walls. The triangles could be grouped in a variety of ways, creating a variety of shapes, and the triangle became the fundamental shape on the building grid. This was seen by some as a radical change because the spaces for learning in schools have been rectangular, and the grid rectilinear.

However, the Dura offers a building that changes classrooms into open spaces, or mixes rooms with open areas. The change was intentional, since independent learning (or self-directed study) is likely to become increasingly important. Open-plan areas suit independent learners, and reconfigurable spaces allow the learning village to adapt to their needs. The hidden potential to remove the barriers in conventional buildings was designed into the Dura. There is even an answer of sorts to the question about the need for schools at all – if the building is no longer needed as a school, it can be recycled for other purposes.

On another level, the vision of a new open space, and open building, offers a new approach to learning (or simply working) – an environment people might like, and might respond to. Even from the outside, the impression is of a building open to the world (see Figures 3.5, 3.6 and 3.7).

The inclusion of trees, and so much space, is indicative of the approach that tries to guarantee a healthy environment – both physically and intellectually. The design is one that shows what can be achieved if the architect is able to go beyond the prejudices of the education system, but it also indicates some of the fundamental assumptions within education that need to be overcome in the move towards better ways of learning.

The Dura is an analogy for learning at a turning point. It is open to the outside world, and the classroom walls that Victorians used like a horse's

Figure 3.6 The learning village: open to the world

Source: courtesy of de Rijke Marsh Morgan architects

blinkers to prevent learners from looking out on the wider world are gone. Rooms can become open spaces where independent individual learning can take place. The Dura's outer structure encloses many largely conventional classrooms (even if they are triangular), but they are created ready to be

Figure 3.7 The learning village: open spaces

Source: courtesy of de Rijke Marsh Morgan architects

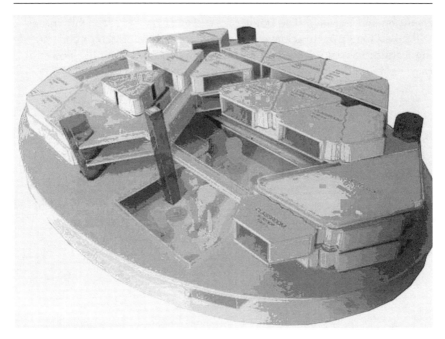

Figure 3.8 The learning village: model of an interior

Source: courtesy of de Rijke Marsh Morgan architects

transformed into another kind of space for another kind of learning. In this light, the Dura can be considered a first attempt at a globalized solution that can be customized to local needs, and to the medium-term evolution in learning.

Change the process

Globalizing learning is about an inevitable process of change. Economic global-ization, the pace of human movement between countries, and other factors will speed the process. Already many years of major research projects have looked specifically at learning in a worldwide context and identified where mistakes have been made and how to make systems more effective. This will not, in itself, solve fundamental problems of educational stagnation. In an age where scientific advances in some areas seem unbelievably fast, it is understandable to look for immediate solutions from pure biochemistry.

However, the scientific quest to understand the human brain in the neuro-scientific context is more challenging than the Human Genome Project (the thirteen-year project coordinated by American national agencies to decode the whole DNA sequence, completed in 2003). It is a quest that has begun to gather momentum and will, inevitably, bring an understanding of human cognition and learning. The staggering extent of the task probably means it will take a long time to achieve. This is not the only approach to understanding learning. Social science methods will help, and – though less powerful – they are more likely to offer a way forward in the short term.

Chapter 4

Education as prejudice

While we're sleeping every night, accountants in India do our taxes. Radiologists in Australia read our CAT scans. And technicians in China build our computers. As other nations race to catch up, there is mounting evidence that American students are falling behind. I know all of you have heard the numbers, but they bear repeating. Currently, our 15-year-olds rank 24th out of 29 developed nations in math literacy and problem solving. Almost half of our 17-year-olds don't have the necessary math skills to work as a production associate at a modern auto plant.

US Secretary of State for Education Spellings'
Prepared Testimony Before the House Committee on
Education and the Workforce, 6 April 2006

Enduring educational prejudice

Education systems are bound by conventional wisdom: they act on tradition, habits and prejudices rather than rigorous evidence. Children learn in certain ways because that is how it has been done in the past, not because there is evidence that these are the best ways to learn. Educationalists operate through prejudice – historical prejudice, true, but prejudice nevertheless. We do not learn from our mistakes: thousands of years of formal education have yet to show much progress in how we teach. It is as meme theory would have it: ideas in education that are popular for whatever reason have a life of their own quite separate from their truth.

The education community presents itself as a model of public service, solely devoted to the needs and aspirations of children and parents, and in touch with the needs of children and society. The reality is that education systems are institutions where there is little pressure to be innovative, or to question how things are done. The prejudices that education systems rely on are all too familiar, for example: standard classrooms; the teacher talking to children; the university lecture; and textbooks. Textbooks, the lecture and repetitive practice – all ways to transmit knowledge – continue to fit conventions established hundreds of years earlier.

From a learner's point of view, too much time is wasted repeating tasks, too much of what is learned is redundant, and there is little social interaction in learning. The primary aim of much education seems to be control: keeping children busy; defining what they must learn and how they must learn; and working towards segregation by educational outcomes. Control is, in educational language, 'discipline', 'rules' and 'classroom management', and the response of children who rebel against the system usually leads to calls for greater controls over children, stricter discipline and even interventions with drugs to make children passive.

One reason for this state of affairs is the long-term persistence of educational prejudices, often in the face of new evidence. There is widespread stagnation and fear of change, with occasional political and media panics about education. These pressures may lead to innovation driven by the need to respond to panics, usually with no sound evidence that they will work. The outcome, if there is permanent change, is that a new prejudice is created.

Why Shakespeare would feel at home in your child's classroom

Early learning occurs primarily in the home where children learn to talk and walk through latent learning and through modelling the behaviour of others. Compared to this sort of development, formal education does little, perhaps because of the means used to make children learn: classrooms, teachers and textbooks.

Figure 4.1 is an image of a classroom like Shakespeare's. Although there are variations, the room would be familiar to children around the world. Historically the classroom was often a room in a house. Despite hundreds of years of development, modern classrooms are still using the same model. There are differences, of course: there is reason to think that Shakespeare had to stand during the day and, like Wordsworth 200 years later, the room would have contained children of different ages. Yet in all essentials, Shakespeare, Wordsworth and many others were educated in a single rectangular room with other children, with the minimum of furniture. The layout is centred around the primary role of a single adult, and the method of communication is mainly verbal (though the blackboard – and whiteboard – are visual). This approach may not be a good one, but at least it is cheap: the main expenditure is the teacher (in schools about three-quarters of all expenditure is on staff, and most of the rest is spent on premises and overheads). Children and university students are lucky if they have even 10 per cent of educational funding spent directly on them and learning resources. This has an impact on the size of learning spaces: classrooms tend to be very small. At the moment in England, the size of a child's classroom is usually about 60 square metres for 30 children and 1 or 2 adults. In effect, a child is expected to work most

Figure 4.1 School for children with sight problems, Prahran, Victoria, about 1890

Source: visionaustralia.org.au

of the day in an area of about 2 square metres, not counting the space that cannot be used because of storage, tables or chairs. In England, you would be arrested if you kept your dog in such a small space for any length of time. And it is not always a nice place to be: the ventilation, heating and furniture are poor in many schools.

The method of delivering learning can be as familiar as the room itself. The teacher, perhaps with other adults, leads the pupils as individuals. The separation of the children from home, family or other people was as real in Shakespeare's time as it is today. The painted walls and lack of equipment are common, and the long hours sustained only by a voice, books and writing are normal. The focus is on the individual, not working with others or improving social skills. What happens in the classroom lies at the heart of most education systems, but one might consider that it is an education system without a heart, where learning is only sometimes an enjoyable experience.

Where in all this is the sense of a lifelong activity, of learning at home, at work and in society at large? It does not exist. Many children are taught subjects and content quite at odds with the skills they will need in later life. The education industry often prides itself on separateness. The needs of society, and of the children themselves, are often sacrificed for education myths.

Inside millions of classrooms, looking out, are the children of today. They do not have control over where they learn, what they learn or how they learn. Many things inside classrooms have not changed for hundreds of years; outside, in the society around them, the rate of change has become dizzyingly fast.

Why teachers don't learn

Inside the classroom stands the teacher, controlling the education of children. Teachers were educated in schoolrooms not unlike the rooms they are teaching in – in fact, many teachers go through school and university, and then go back into school and university. The apprenticeship model through which teachers learn to be teachers may indicate one of the reasons why education systems are so slow to change. Teachers are taught to imitate the practice of other teachers, within slowly evolving policy frameworks or reforms. Teachers are not necessarily against change, or ill-disposed to improvement – quite the contrary. But the task they face every day, given the support they have in the task of educating children, is impossible. Even the most dedicated teacher cannot invent excellent experiences for every child every minute of the day. Like being an absolute monarch, the position of teacher is not one that could be fulfilled to perfection by any human being.

An easy analogy to bring this point home is that of a family. Imagine you had 30 children (and all at once and of the same age – since children in classes are usually the same age) and your husband or wife said, 'Take them into that big room over there and help them learn something useful every day for five hours a day. I'll be checking up on you. And no, you don't have much money to spend – there are other priorities.' You might struggle to teach them all to read, prepare them for life and employment, and stay sane yourself. It would probably not work to say to them, 'Do this because it will help you in ten years' time to get a good job' or 'This is what you need to know for an important examination to get you into university' and to expect them to behave perfectly and enjoy learning all the time. Sometimes they might even argue with one another, or get upset and need comforting, or simply be hard to control. The tendency to play it safe as a teacher is understandable: if you know your job is impossible to do perfectly, then there is safety in what you know will get you through the day.

Teachers do not, as a rule, carefully evaluate the effectiveness of what they do. A recent attempt to create an evidence base of what teachers did came to the uninspiring conclusion: 'This systematic review was commissioned by the Teacher Training Agency . . . examining relevant literature, there was evidence that *"teachers adopt strategies based on ideology, common sense or school based effectiveness but rarely on evaluated effectiveness"*.'

The mindset of teachers is one that looks to what they already know: unproven theories, traditional approaches (labelled 'common sense') or school beliefs of what is effective (ideas of their colleagues). They only rarely look at the evidence, because few are supported by their school even if they do: they are confined by conventional wisdom. So for the teacher, as for the children in the classroom, the routines of the education system continue year after year. These routines may slowly evolve, but they do so in response to theories, traditions and professional trends rather than evidence. It is not just the children who are trapped.

Myths: why children can't write properly

Few people know how to write and speak grammatically – or so many of us are led to think by some educationalists. Everyone has educational illusions like this, and teachers do too. For the last 100 years many teachers and self-proclaimed experts have believed that children will write better English if they are taught grammar. It seems to make sense to them – if you know the rules and the system, you will do it better. Unfortunately 100 years of research has shown that teaching abstract, formal grammar systems makes children's writing worse – and certainly no better. Yet teachers and others refuse to accept the evidence (if they even know about it), believing the myth of grammar teaching. They continue to support it, they continue to teach it, and researchers continue to investigate. The results continue to be the same – grammar teaching does not improve children's writing.

This is despite the embarrassing discovery for supporters of grammar teaching that the grammar they advocate – a set of rules that has been in use in various grammar textbooks for hundreds of years – is not the grammar of any language. Noam Chomsky showed that all languages and all grammars are based on deep structure. The key difference he points to is that language is a way of communicating our thoughts. Some language experts use the term 'mentalese' (instead of thought) to describe the representation of concepts and propositions in the brain (including those for the meaning of words and sentences). In other terms, we have ideas in our brain that we try to communicate – and sometimes find very hard to communicate – through language. The structures we use to embody our thoughts in language are, in all languages, broadly alike, though the deep structure is really uncompromisingly logical as those who have grappled with Chomsky's model will know (one of the reasons deep structure is not a useful system to teach to children). Chomsky asserts that all people acquire the ability to carry out this process without formal teaching, and some have speculated that it must, therefore, be a reflection of the physical pathways in the brain.

Another real problem with the grammar myth is that grammar appears to be a disposition to acquire language skills in all people – an instinct of sorts according to some, but in reality a neurologically based process. The interaction of two areas of the brain – Wernicke's area (associated with meaning) and Broca's area (associated with syntax) – is fundamental in acquiring language skills, and this interaction occurs early. Children have, by the age of 5, a clear syntactical sense. They acquire it without being directly taught grammar, but largely through latent learning, and it is a useful illustration of the ability to learn multifaceted processes without being taught in a declarative, formal way. A child's grammar is different in a variety of ways from the language of print, because it is the grammar of ordinary speech, and reading skills are fully established later – in fact, the skill of reading changes their brain activity. Telling a child that their spoken grammar is wrong and that they should use a set of rules based on many teachers' misunderstanding of grammar will not help to improve their writing.

A more likely explanation of why grammar teaching does not improve writing is simply that children are disposed to learning grammars by assimilating other people's structures: first in speech, and then, for formal prose, by reading. In other words, they learn by example, and do not deduce how to use language from a set of abstract, formal rules: this is deduction, whereas all their grammar sense is developed by induction and modelling others. More reading and listening to examples of formal prose might be a more appropriate way to improve their writing.

The sad reality remains that formal grammar still is taught as a method of improving writing and that millions of hours of children's lives are wasted – and their writing even harmed – by this:

> The results of the present in-depth review point to one clear conclusion: that there is no high quality evidence to counter the prevailing belief that the teaching of the principles underlying and informing word order or 'syntax' has virtually no influence on the writing quality or accuracy of 5 to 16 year olds. This conclusion remains the case whether the syntax teaching is based on the 'traditional' approach of emphasising word order and parts of speech, or on the 'transformational' approach, which is based on generative-transformational grammar.
>
> (EPPI, Anderson *et al*.: 4)

Yet such is the power of conventional wisdom in education that many governments still insist that grammar is taught to all children, most education systems make it a requirement, and society at large is conditioned to think it is necessary.

Why textbook answers are wrong

Day-to-day education systems are, on some levels, about control. Much of the work set in schools and other education institutions is intended to keep learners busy, and these tasks are often embedded in textbooks. The quality of textbooks varies a great deal, but they are often unappealing as a learning experience, a fact that can be demonstrated by asking two questions: 'Have you ever read a textbook for fun?' and 'Have you ever had your interest in a certain subject destroyed by textbooks?'. It is not surprising that textbooks are dull, since the education system has created its own books that do not have to compete in the wider market. Much of children's time in school is spent practising from textbook tasks rather than learning. These books often give small bits of information, followed by repetitive tasks that keep children busy, aimed at short, lesson-length time slots. Even copying out of textbooks is far from a forgotten practice, and plagiarism – copying out of books or from friends or from the internet instead of writing an essay yourself – is common in most education systems.

Like teachers learning how to teach from older teachers, textbooks are modelled on previous textbooks, and authored by teachers and lecturers in their spare time. They are often created from the adult's own notes on a subject and exercises they have given students – hence textbooks tend to reinforce what already happens in classrooms. In many ways textbooks contribute to conventional wisdom but do not necessarily make a good contribution to educating people. They have many faults, such as a tendency to present all information as unquestionably correct, using didactic, unattractive prose. Some textbooks leave a great deal more to be desired. The American Association for the Advancement of Science (AAAS) carried out a review of textbooks, and concluded that part of the weaknesses in American mathematics teaching was a result of the textbooks and how they impacted on learning: 'While there are undoubtedly multiple and complex reasons for this, and no simple remedies, the instructional materials used in the schools are a substantial part of the problem.'

The evaluation of science textbooks in Project 2061 (which looked at the possible state of Science in the US at that date) was even more damning as it focused on issues of accuracy as well as adequacy, and concluded that there were simple errors of fact in science textbooks. The quality of textbooks as instructional aids was poor:

> Not one of the widely used science textbooks for middle school was rated satisfactory by Project 2061, the long-term science, mathematics, and technology education reform initiative of the American Association for the Advancement of Science (AAAS) [which reported:] 'Our students are lugging home heavy texts full of disconnected facts that neither educate nor motivate them,' said Dr George Nelson, Director of Project 2061. 'It's a credit to science teachers that their students are learning anything at all. No matter how "scientifically accurate" a text may be,' Nelson continued, 'if it doesn't provide teachers and students with the right kinds of help in understanding and applying important concepts, then it's not doing its job.'
>
> (Project 2061, press notice)

The simple message was that all commercially available textbooks were unsatisfactory, and there were worrying limitations in every area assessed (see Figure 4.2). There was only one book that was rated satisfactory and that covered only part of the course – physical science. The American Association for the Advancement of Science is hardly a radical institution, but the inadequacy of the textbooks used across the US has led to their attack on the low quality of educational publishing in many areas.

Textbooks are also subject to political control – not all of which is as humorous as the fate of a Rajasthani textbook. The book:

> compares politicians unfavourably to donkeys [and] is to have the offending chapter removed, following complaints from aggrieved politicians. Rajasthan's education minister Ghanshyam Tiwari failed to persuade members of the state assembly that the chapter was nothing more than satire . . . Complaints about the book have only just surfaced, even though it has been in use for a year.
>
> (BBC News Online: 4 April 2006)

Nor should the impact of textbooks on the economy be underrated – for example, one of the largest publishers on earth is the Mexican Ministry of Education – nor the impact on the students themselves: 'In some countries a rule of thumb is pupils' bags should not weigh more than 10% of their body weight. In N[orthern] I[reland] they are often carrying much more than that.'

The textbook is, after the teacher, probably the dominant method of knowledge transmission in schools, but in universities the lecture is still important. It is a very old model. Yet lectures are, at their best, an excellent source of understanding and knowledge. The trouble with good lectures is that they take so long to compose. Like textbooks, the composition of lectures takes many weeks – and a lifetime of study. Most people cannot achieve an excellent lecture. And no one can achieve that excellence lecture after lecture. This is a fundamental problem in communication: can any of us produce something interesting and informative to say every time we speak? The failures of education are not all because we still use lectures or textbooks. It is because almost all lectures, books, digital programs and verbal interactions do not embody the human investment necessary to make them classic learning experiences.

Are new methods the solution? From radio to television, from television to computers, people have hoped that a change of media would enliven education in schools and replace textbooks and lectures. At the moment, it is fairly clear that these hopes are false. Television and digital learning are even more expensive and time consuming to create than lectures and books. Unless the human input into these learning products is very high indeed, we are just making mass media ways of transmitting second-rate lectures or textbooks.

Textbooks graded by AAAS Project 2061: Middle Grades Science Textbook Evaluation	Rating of Instructional Quality (average rating for physical science)					
	Unsatisfactory (0–1.9)				Satisfactory (2.0–3.0)	
Glencoe Life, Earth and Physical Science (1997)			▓			
Macmillan/McGraw-Hill Science (1995)		▓				
Middle School Science and Technology (1999)			▓			
Prentice Hall Science (1997)		▓				
Prime Science (1998)			▓			
Science (2000)			▓			
Science Insights (1997)		▓				
Science Interactions (1998)			▓			
Science Plus: Technology and Society (1997)			▓			
Matter and Molecules (Michigan State University, 1998)					▓	

Figure 4.2 AAAS Project 2061: middle grades science textbooks evaluation

Source: American Association for the Advancement of Science, modified by the author

The art of distilling human knowledge, understanding and skills is not easily achieved, and a low investment approach through textbooks or lectures suitable only for a limited audience is not the way to achieve it. Simply using new technology will not make the content better. The task is not made easier because of the huge growth in knowledge – every day the task of communicating what is known becomes more challenging. And every day, a billion people endure an approach to learning fixated on classrooms, teachers and textbooks.

Marks out of ten

What most parents want to know about their children is whether they are making progress, whether they have any special talent or problems, whether they are getting on well with others, happy, healthy – and what they as parents can do to help them. These seem the right questions to ask. Education systems tend to judge children in relation to others – ignoring vital areas such as social skills, health and self-concept. An extreme example of a simplistic approach to assessment is the English National Curriculum assessing every child up to the age of 14 in every subject on a scale of 1 to 10 (a child of 5 is 'working towards Level 1', and most children at 14 only get to Level 5 or 6). In this system it can take years for a child to move up a level. Such crude assessment is nonsense, but people take these numbers seriously, because people tend to believe educational judgements.

The real question is not just whether such examinations and tests work well. The question is more serious: what do they do to children? Testing every child has, overall, a negative effect on the learning outcomes and attitudes of children. Government reforms that change the examinations or tests allow researchers to make large-scale, rigorous assessments of the impact of new forms of measurement. Key examples are from England and the US, where new tests generated huge data sets. A rigorous analysis of the data showed that tests and practice tests tend to make children who do not do well lose self-esteem and, in the end, do less well in school. More specifically, the drive for educational accountability in each US state's education system led to a highly undesirable outcome: 'the state-mandated tests in the US lower self-esteem for "at risk" students.' The very people that education systems should give the greatest support to were being damaged, yet this kind of impact is a well-known consequence of large-scale competitive testing. It is an effect that also occurred in England where national tests are carried out at 7, 11 and 14: 'After the introduction of the National Curriculum Tests in England, low-achieving pupils had lower self-esteem than higher-achieving pupils, whilst beforehand there was no correlation between self-esteem and achievement.'

Repeated practice tests reinforced the low self-image of the lower-achieving students. Students were aware of the classroom focus on tests, and that the tests concentrated on a narrow view of what they could do. Many children disliked high-stakes tests, showed high levels of test anxiety (particularly girls) and preferred other forms of assessment. The feedback from teachers often hurt children's feelings rather than helping them understand their weaknesses. Children often responded by reducing their effort towards further learning and focusing on performance in tests.

The testing also had an impact on the nature of children's learning: 'teachers adopt a teaching style which emphasizes transmission teaching of knowledge', an approach 'favouring those students who prefer to learn in this way and disadvantaging and lowering the self-esteem of those who prefer more active and creative learning experiences'.

It is not possible to say that this is the impact of examination systems generally at every age, but it seems as if these new examinations had a range of potentially damaging effects beyond inhibiting children's learning: 'An education system that puts great emphasis on evaluation produces students with strong extrinsic orientation towards grades and social status.'

There were alternative approaches, where interest and effort were encouraged in classrooms, and there was self-regulated learning by providing students with an element of choice, control over challenge and opportunities to work collaboratively. The research suggested a number of actions, one of which was simple – 'avoid comparisons between students based on test results', a piece of advice no government has yet taken – and the other a fundamental point about measurement in education – the limitations of assessment: 'present assessment realistically, as a process which is inherently imprecise . . . with results that have to be regarded as tentative and indicative rather than definitive.'

It is a simple point, but one that confirms what most people already know in their hearts: educational tests, grades, examinations and assessments are not the accurate, fair and necessary part of education systems they are presented to be by the education industry. This fixation on such outcomes is, however, rather missing the point. The way outcomes are measured (which is poor and imprecise anyway), and the use they are put to (to categorize individuals), reflect a system that has lost its way. Even children complain about memorizing content just for examinations, knowing they will rapidly forget most of it after the examination is over. Examination systems do not help children learn – which is, in the end, the purpose of education systems in the first place.

Myths: why children are violent

The emotional and social development of young people is not central to education systems. Civics and citizenship exist at the fringes of most formal education, along with some attempt to address the soft skills of human interaction. They disappear in universities. Meanwhile stories about the poor behaviour of young people appear in the media everywhere on earth, though never linked to the impersonal and judgemental educational experience that might, in part, account for it.

In the US, the media attention on violent young people became intense after the mass murders of young people in school or university (as in Virginia in 2007). 'Media panic' is an apt description of the response, which tended towards apocalyptic prose at times. More sophisticated responses to such events, such as Michael Moore's *Bowling for Columbine*, were rare. The US Surgeon General's Report *Youth Violence* is, perhaps, the most combative governmental response to media panics about young people in recent years.

The fundamental argument of the Surgeon General's report is that public perceptions are a barrier to progress and that it is therefore necessary to 'challenge false notions and misconceptions about youth violence'. *Youth Violence* goes so far as to assert that 'damaging myths and stereotypes that interfere with the task at hand' are contributing factors themselves. The report lists some of the most common myths, although some of the myths seem very American:

- African American and Hispanic youths are more likely to become involved in violence than other racial or ethnic groups.
- A new, violent breed of young super-predators threatens the United States.

Most of these myths are the stuff of media reports – and popular solutions – around the world:

- Getting tough with juvenile offenders by trying them in adult criminal courts reduces the likelihood that they will commit more crimes.
- Nothing works with respect to treating or preventing violent behaviour.
- Most violent youths will end up being arrested for a violent crime.

The report is upbeat about the potential to improve the situation, arguing that 'youth violence is not an intractable problem'. It sees patterns of violence as a continuum, where solutions can 'reduce or even prevent much of the most serious youth violence . . . reducing less dangerous, but still serious problem behaviors and promoting healthy development'. It is adamant that the real problem is the way we are tackling violence, given that 'schools nationwide are relatively safe'. *Youth Violence* argues for a social sciences approach to confront the issues systematically, using valid research methodologies and acting from knowledge – not conventional wisdom. There are solutions, such as working with all the people that a child is in contact with, taking a social rather than an individual approach, using intervention programmes rather than prison, ensuring rigorous evaluation and quality delivery of programmes, and tackling conventional wisdom.

Of course, the report has weaknesses from a non-US point of view: it does not directly address the root cause of gun crime – the easy access to guns. In that respect it reflects the Surgeon General's report on obesity, which does not tackle the food industry's contribution to the obesity problem. Nevertheless *Youth Violence* does have lessons for most countries (and media organizations): that the myths are nothing more than myths; that it is possible to intervene and improve things rather than imprison young people; and that there are solutions that arise from a different approach to children. Naturally, the report has had little impact – conventional wisdom about young people is unlikely to be swayed by a single report, however reputable and well researched.

Prejudice, media panics and panaceas

In a land where ignorance is king, the media and charlatans posing as experts are princes. This is true in education. Prejudices die hard, and too few people are committed to improvement based on rigorous social scientific (and neuroscientific) evidence. In the meantime we are distracted by media panics about some perceived education issue, or by charlatans who tell us there is a simple solution in order to promote themselves or their solutions.

It seems Galbraith was right about the power of conventional wisdom where there is no powerful scientific community in place. In such situations, he argued, the acceptability of ideas, rather than their truth, would dominate because in such circumstances people 'associate truth with convenience –

with what most closely accords with self-interest and personal well-being or promises best to avoid awkward effort or unwelcome dislocation of life'.

Decisions in education are often driven by the self-interest of educators, educational institutions, politicians and parents. People do not really consider education systems from a child's point of view. Like other people, young people want a nice place to work; a friendly, social atmosphere; good resources; enjoyable, valuable experiences; and work that involves something useful or that they want to accomplish. They like an efficient use of their time, some freedom and flexibility, and even rewards – all the things adults want in their own lives and in their own homes, perhaps. Above all, young people want to be treated as fellow human beings, not as a race apart. Such goals are not impractical, and they are achievable. Although there are many things that are wrong with the way children are educated, many people are afraid of change: it could disrupt children's education; it could go wrong; adults have survived their education, so children can survive. There are many reasons to be fearful when there is no good-quality evidence. A safe starting point is to change the way we approach change, by adopting a truly scientific approach – a tried and tested methodology. Conventional wisdom is, in the end, what we should be afraid of:

> These false ideas are intrinsically dangerous. Assumptions that a problem does not exist or failure to recognize the true nature of a problem can obscure the need for informed policy or for interventions. An example is the conventional wisdom in many circles that the epidemic of youth violence so evident in the early 1990s is over. Alternatively, myths may trigger public fears and lead to inappropriate or misguided policies that result in inefficient or counterproductive use of scarce public resources.
>
> (*Youth Violence*: 9)

Chapter 5

Learning from mistakes

All human institutions are imperfect, and the challenge for each is to learn from the successes and failures.

Joseph Stiglitz, *Making Globalization Work*

Learning from mistakes

The variety of education systems has created a natural experiment: to control that experiment, and learn from it, is a fundamental starting point for improvement. There are now rigorous social science methods, using major advances in statistical analysis and ICT, able to implement large-scale, international and comparative studies to identify mistakes – as well as what appears to work well. The confidence in these new methodologies should not blind us to the potential pitfalls. The calls for a social science approach to education systems is over 100 years old and is strongly supported by social scientists – as one might imagine. The vast majority of educational research carried out in the past is not good enough – parents, educationalists and employers rightly distrust any sentence that begins, 'Research shows . . .' because of the poor quality of research used to justify almost anything in education. Against this is the rhetoric of the rigorous research community that is visionary, though the reality has been, at times, disappointing.

The US's National Educational Research Policy and Priorities Board, for example, argues that research must improve, otherwise 'American students will never learn as much as they might. And our schools will never be as good as they can be'. This conclusion was reached after a five-year consultation with a range of stakeholders, and focused on America, though it seems a truism that has international application. The same report asserts:

We argue that research, broadly defined, is the nation's most powerful instrument for improving student achievement. We lay out a vision of schools for the future in which *all* American children are learning at world-class levels. We establish reading, mathematics, and second-language learning as the north stars by which we guide a focused, high-quality, and practical research programme for the next decade.

(NERPPB: 2)

It would be churlish to criticize either the ambition or the ability of social science to make a significant contribution to improvement. But a week is a long time in politics, a year is a long time in a child's life and a governmental programme that lasts a decade after a five-year consultation is a rare beast indeed. The potential of rigorous social science to drive change is real, but the process has to be quicker, cheaper and better than it has been to date.

Governments in many countries are trying to assess their education systems. Most use old, non-rigorous methods – what might be called the 'Ministry of Education' model. This approach relies on inspectors or education experts, who visit schools, talk to people, examine data in a traditional way, commission small-scale research projects, write reports and make recommendations. The UK's Office for Standards in Education (OFSTED) is an example, and India's Inspectorate is another. This old-fashioned, bureaucratic, non-scientific approach is – broadly speaking – totally useless, except for the inspirational insights of individuals. The new wave of rigorous research by teams of social scientists using advanced statistical techniques is, in contrast, a valuable approach to identifying our mistakes. One strand of this research is carried out by organizations such as the OECD, using new methods to compare educational achievement in countries worldwide. A second strand is reviewing all the educational research of the past to find any research that meets new, rigorous quality standards. The outcomes are often meta-analyses, bringing together all the research on a single topic and drawing general conclusions from the best research. Finally, there are a group of researchers who combine the two approaches of international/comparative studies and rigorous experimental methods to look at what really works in schools (sometimes called 'effectiveness' research). This research approach aims to identify mistakes and identify better alternatives. The combination of these research approaches means that there is a sound way forward to make schools more effective. This has to be tempered with a realization that these methods concentrate on the analysis of education as it is and identify what is most effective – they do not create new solutions. Yet, at last, there is light at the end of the tunnel.

Rigorous research like this can help make schools more effective by cutting through the jargon and fads of educational policy to the real effects on learners. For example, there has been the notion that leaders in education drive improvement in schools much as it is argued that leaders in industry drive improvement in industry. A great deal of attention has been devoted to leaders such as Maine's Academy for School Leaders or the UK's National College of School Leadership. A large body of poor research has been carried out worldwide: for example, the US's Education Resources Information Centre cites 2,517 articles on 'leadership effectiveness'. These articles make many assertions, such as the 'paramount' importance of school principals or the strong direct links between improved leadership and improved student performance. The University of London's Evidence for Policy and Practice Information and Co-ordinating Centre (EPPI Centre) analysed the research and the 'widespread, strongly held belief' that school leadership makes a big difference. Their conclusions did not support the belief that improving leadership was a panacea, rather – as one might suspect – that it was a small element in good education:

> The evidence relating to the effect of headteachers on student outcomes indicates that such an effect is largely indirect. It is mediated through key intermediate factors, these being the work of teachers, the organisation of the school, and relationship with parents and the wider community . . . Hence one tentative conclusion from these findings is to suggest that leadership that is distributed among the wider school staff might be more likely to have an effect on the positive achievement of student outcomes than that which is largely, or exclusively, 'top-down'.
>
> (EPPI, Bell *et al.*: 3)

The conclusions counteract the exaggerated rhetoric about the influence of leaders, suggesting leadership is a quality many people in an organization might show to good effect (as, one suspects, is true in almost any organization). Care is taken when suggesting a possible line of action ('one tentative conclusion'), but as a whole the report offers a rigorous, mediated view of research that is a more trustworthy judgement than was previously available. It is one example of good research methodologies in practice and how they can be used to help institutions recognize mistakes.

Effective starting points

The immediate issue in improving education, whatever the long term might be, is how to make the most effective use of the resources and systems already in place. The rigorous research that has been carried out to date has tended to focus on the teacher, partly because the conventional wisdom is that the teacher is the single most important person in the learning space. The idea that learning is so dependent on the teacher or lecturer is both short sighted and limiting. Nevertheless, the effective school researchers offer useful insights that, in essence, argue that teachers need to work efficiently and effectively, and the general conclusions are ones that probably apply to formal learning whether in homes, school, university or work.

The most important research finding in effectiveness research is that active teaching and variety are essential, where the teacher constantly interacts with the learners with questions, exposition, dialogue and demonstration. In simple terms, the teacher needs to maximize their impact on learners through active engagement with them as a class, group or individual. What applies to teachers applies to anyone helping a child learn (parents, trainers and other children). For parents this approach is often called 'quality time': a total focus on the child. An interesting extension is peer teaching or coaching (where children teach each other), and research suggests the same need to be active is true. Active teaching makes sense: anyone helping a child learn is likely to make a higher impact because, in effect, they are making a greater effort.

Examining exactly what activities best contribute to active teaching reveals something of the principles. The first is clarity about what the goals are: a 'strong mission', a clear lesson structure, focused questioning and exposition on the aims (which should be specific rather than too general), and keeping the focus of the classroom interactions on these goals. The second feature is the high interaction with the learners, in terms of questioning, how the lesson is delivered, using the children's ideas, probing for knowledge and – on a human level – knowing them (and their names, level of understanding and their ways of learning). A well-known example of this is persistent questioning where, in Japan, teachers will often ask six or seven questions of a child. The third feature is effective time management of the lesson, using well-established routines and making sure high levels of children's time are spent working as directed. Finally, active teaching is characterized by incentives: high expectations of what pupils can achieve, high success rate for pupils (75–80 per cent succeeding), frequent positive feedback, and – linked to this – corrective instruction and feedback. These general features are indicative of good interactive teaching though not a recipe for learning for all children all of the time. There are questions about how effective a single teacher can be in terms of such an approach. The learning in a classroom, however focused, is only approximating the best way forward for each individual child.

There are other people who are central to learning: parents, peers, others – not just teachers. The way in which those people communicate with the learner can also be positive and intense, and indirectly have the features identified by effectiveness research. This makes sense: a real focus on a child and their developing understanding of an area of knowledge leads to an intense interaction that is at the heart of learning. The people involved can be in a different emotional and social relationship with the child, and this is a very significant difference: all learning is social, but its nature and effectiveness depend on the web of personal relationships in which it takes place.

It is not surprising then that one effectiveness indicator clearly links school, home, social and work learning: a warm, supportive classroom climate has been shown to impact directly on children's learning. Many people respond as if this is an obvious truth. However, the role of positive human feeling in learning is not particularly emphasized in schools, and external evaluations often talk of teachers managing the children well, rather than creating a positive emotional climate. Some work-based and school environments seem to accept neutral or negative climates as acceptable, while homes and social environments are supposed to be warm and supportive. It is recognized that poor climates in homes have a negative impact, and it is true in schools and other learning environments. Creating a warm, supportive environment is one of a teacher's most valuable talents, even if it only makes their teaching more effective.

Economic lessons

The resources used in education systems and in learning generally (whether textbooks, books, video or digital resources) are actually very important, and often largely ignored in drives to improve education systems. They are even less likely to be subject to rigorous evaluation – unless they are something different from a traditional textbook, such as educational television in the 1970s. Ignoring the actual learning materials that people use (and the influence of books and other media outside the classroom) is inexplicable. However, it does offer the opportunity to create a richer learning environment for everyone by improving such resources for learning.

In the past, it was always the case that the poor could not have access to the learning resources of the rich. The price of a book in the 1800s might be far beyond the means of those wishing to read it; newspapers in the 1850s when Dickens was writing were often read aloud to groups of people simply because they were expensive, and the revolution of modern technologies such as the internet has had an uneven impact on society and the children within it – the so-called digital divide. The aspirational target in many countries is for children to have access to the internet, and projects such as the Gutenberg Project (which publishes some of the most important texts of all time online) aim to bring every child a library equal to any in any school. The simple economics of the internet are that a connection to the internet and a device that displays print will ensure access to a library that would cost hundreds of thousands of dollars in print. So there is a very reasonable expectation that, in due course, the historical library of texts will become available to all learners. This is a starting point, but only that: a learning experience can go beyond just having access to a good library.

Resources for learning have greater impact if they are attractive, functional, and focused on key learning objectives in a sequence that supports the learner's growing understanding. In the commercial world, important new products are created and market tested to improve them before they are sold, usually using sophisticated social science techniques. Then they are constantly evaluated in order to improve them and to continue the process of gaining market share – and profits. The production of a new car is even more analytical, since very different elements, from ergonomics to environmental impact, as well as the interrelationships between vehicle technologies and aesthetic design, have to be considered. The investment in a product as it is created should also apply to the making of minds. In broad terms, the commercial high investment approach could create excellent learning resources aimed at everyone from young children to engineers involved in medical technology. In the US, the Institute of Educational Science has spurred on initiatives for evaluating digital resources and interventions. Predictably, most commercial products fail to show a real impact on learning in rigorous research analysis, as almost all such products did not invest in market testing or related quality assurance processes. On the other hand, the thoughtful creation of books, television, internet sites and digital resources has created some excellent learning materials. The investment in such resources is vital because their impact is not simply a question of effectiveness but is also an investment in the art of making learning attractive. The days of the amateur textbook model – where teachers simply reproduced newer versions of the same thing – will come to an end: as the economic value of learning rises, better methods of content production and better delivery will, in the end, dominate.

There is potential for a global market in learning resources. Such resources are suitable for an international approach: there are economies of scale through varying the language of a resource; and the resource can be flexible if created and stored in a digital format. There may be difficult decisions for countries such as Latvia that are not in a position to invest heavily in home-produced materials, and for learning to flourish in such small markets the alternatives are widespread translation from other sources – or delivering learning in another language. These stark choices reflect learning realities that are essentially the acknowledged business realities of the twenty-first century. In such a global perspective digital resources have many attractions: they can be modified in real time to improve the resource, they can be versioned into any language and the distribution costs are usually very low.

All of this might seem an impossible goal, but it is, in fact, happening all around us. Software products such as Microsoft Office are an example of the same process: a learning resource that is in use in different linguistic and cultural environments. The products become more functional, too: different language versions, dictionaries and spell checks are re-used as translation resources. Ideally resources must be accurate, up to date and have all the strengths of good communication: clarity, precision and brevity. Software companies use the behaviour and feedback from customers to identify weaknesses and try to correct them. This process of product creation and globalizing its functionality is, of course, commercial: it creates a bigger market, and, in general, a continually improving product will make more money. This approach is, however, very effective in helping people to learn to use (and become attached to or dependent on) the product: it is a model learning resources can copy. The investment in creating such resources is high, which is why it would normally require a team of authors, media technologists and researchers working full time to create this kind of learning resource. Again, this may seem a distant dream, though in fact it happens already in many of the courses of the Open University. The vital role of knowledge mediation and presentation in learning resources should not be underestimated: learners need to be engaged through such resources, and not just able to learn from them if they are highly motivated. The role of the popularizers of learning is more important in education than it is in most other areas of human activity: the transfer of knowledge is not just a question of telling another generation, it is important to engage that generation's interest.

The technological revolution is also changing the devices for learning. There is a drive towards personal and home digital devices uniting many functionalities. Mobile phones, iPods, digital cameras, hand-held televisions, gaming devices and laptops are beginning to blur into a single device (with high-quality screens that display books with the same quality as paper – an important, if largely ignored, development). Equally, the functionalities of those devices are converging to include entertainment, information, communication, internet, interactivity and creation tools including word processing, data analysis and so on. This convergence offers another powerful platform for learning, communication and entertainment rather than keeping an artificial division between such functions. It creates a rich environment for home, work and formal education, where the production costs of resources is reduced as the distribution costs fall. 'Edutainment' is a dismissive description of popularizing learning, but in principle it is a vital contribution to the improvement of learning. The coming together of different technologies to give fewer devices with greater functionality is not a long-term aspiration – it is beginning to happen – as is a single platform that can be shared between entertainment, employment and education, a process to create good products and services in all three areas, and the tendency towards globalization.

The description above of the qualities learning resources should have is, however, only partial. The more challenging elements are those that mimic the contribution of good teachers to learning: managing to create a clear learning focus; being highly interactive and responsive to the learner; managing time well (being efficient); offering incentives, rapid feedback and success; and, finally, offering a warm, human environment. From this, it is possible to understand the attraction of gaming technologies as a possible tool for learning. However, no current technology or device can completely replace the need for humans, and for social interaction in learning. The potential marketplace for learning in technological environments is being created, and there are significant economic drivers for individuals and families to invest.

Making connections

Before considering the economic forces for investment in learning, it might be useful to consider how new kinds of learning experiences might be created for such an environment. There are, of course, traditional products, such as distance learning packages from current providers. However, either a large private-sector organization (say, a major software provider in entertainment) or a public-sector organization (such as a wealthy university) might consider how to approach the problem from first principles. Such an organization would have the capacity to create learning experiences using teams for creating resources, existing quality assurance systems, advanced development methodologies and marketing expertise.

The evolution of learning resources is becoming quite rapid. My own experience of the process is, perhaps, an illustration. In 1985 when I edited the scripts of David Leland's television quartet, *Tales out of School* (Cambridge University Press), its publication was quite conventional: an introduction and then a script. The only innovation was the sale of the video alongside the book and the package's use in a national examination. In 1992 for *A Midsummer Night's Dream* (Cambridge University Press) there was more support alongside Shakespeare's script: images, glossaries, running plot summaries and even diagrams, as well as the traditional introduction. In 1999 *Writers' Workshop* was a major departure: a digital resource with text, sound, images, video, interactivity, creative tools (for sound tracks or radio programmes) and a languages switch that changed everything from English to French, German or Spanish. *Writers' Workshop* (Granada Media) was created to be versioned into minority languages, and in due course it was – into Irish. All of those publications were single resources sold by large organizations. In contrast, in 2003 a team of teachers led by Mike Butler at Monkseaton High School created a course covering language lessons from age 7 to age 11 in French, Spanish, German, English and Mandarin. The course included all the learning materials needed, how to deliver them and training for the teacher, and was distributed in digital format. The uptake was impressive – over 1,200 schools to date – and the cost was less than $1 per pupil. In addition, there was inbuilt self-assessment for the students that acted as a quality control mechanism for the resource. The learning outcomes from the course are good, and the money raised by selling it is being used to improve the course – with the French course already in its second version. The evolution from a book for an exam, a small part of a set curriculum, to a digital resource that does not need exams and defines its own curriculum was complete.

Changes in the nature of resources need to be linked to changes in the nature of learning itself: a device that offers all manner of content and has powerful tools for creative learning and work contexts would need to link to people and defined outcomes to become a powerful new way of learning. Many people feel unsure of educational change that involves radical departures from historical models. Consider your instinctive reaction to a course based on the following approach:

Student-centred learning
During their school education, students are normally told by their teacher which topics will be taught and how they should learn them. With 'student-centred' learning, it is the students who will identify areas that

they are not wholly familiar with and take greater responsibility for the way in which they learn.

Problem-based learning

Problem-based learning (PBL) is an educational process that encourages students to learn through curiosity and to seek out information for themselves. Why use PBL? Traditional programmes have been criticized for encouraging students to acquire knowledge without understanding how it is applied in practice. PBL increases students' understanding by linking basic science with practice early in the programme, so that interest is stimulated and maintained. PBL develops lifelong learning skills. To keep pace with the rapid rate of change in science, people need to update their knowledge continuously and know how to apply it. The skills students acquire through PBL will help them to continue learning and applying their knowledge throughout their careers: students identify their own learning needs; students take responsibility for their own learning. [edited]

Many people's responses would be to accept the worthy intentions but question the effectiveness and practicality of such a programme, especially when the details of the process are clear:

Structure of a typical PBL module: small groups of six or seven students meet with their teachers where a relevant scenario, 'the problem', is presented; the group explores the problem by applying their prior knowledge and identifying areas about which they need to learn more; teachers provide guidance during the tutorial; students leave the meeting with group learning objectives which are used as the framework for study; there is great use made of independent study: students achieve their learning objectives by using a variety of learning resources. [edited]

There are a number of distinctive features of this approach: the students determine the curriculum, are independent, use a range of resources, and the process stresses a procedural approach and applications of knowledge. It is actually the highly respected approach to Medicine at Liverpool University, praised by the UK's Quality Assurance Agency as 'very effective development and delivery of a highly innovative problem-based undergraduate curriculum . . . [students are] enthusiastic, reflective and active learners'. The course, like most medical courses, requires skills in reading images and photographs, being able to acquire fine motor skills, and the learning skills to keep up to date with new scientific and medical knowledge: a model, if you will, of good learning in a rapidly evolving field. The approach to learning adopted by Liverpool University's School of Medical Education is one that suits learning where the resources support procedural methods: a model that is ideal for new technologies.

Learning that is based on the functionality of the brain is likely to be more effective, a point that is not lost on those beginning to create more effective ways to learn. The neural patterns in the brain are a network that is, in one analogy, not unlike the internet, where each computer is a node of information and processing, and the internet connections are the pathways between these nodes. Information flows through the system in many different ways. The brain is at once both more and less precise than this: it has a modular structure fulfilling different functions through nodes and pathways within each module. However, higher-order cognition often depends on activating pathways between these modules, in what might be termed creative ways. These pathways are created or enhanced by stimulation – impulses travelling through obscure but existing pathways meet in unrelated modules and in so doing both enhance the pathways down which they travelled and promote the creation of new, obscure pathways. In simple terms, you have to start thinking in a new way in order to create new pathways – or 'cells that fire together, wire together'. This linking of different modules of the brain, creating pathways that can be strengthened – and repeated – is fundamental to higher-order thinking. The descriptions of the Liverpool medical course above mirror this neuroscientific process, perhaps not entirely by accident: 'Problem Based Learning increases students' understanding by linking basic science with medical practice early in the programme, so that interest is stimulated and maintained.' The links within and between modules in the brain reflect the plasticity of the brain – the ability for it to adapt to the environment. From the perspective of learning the emphasis is clearly on process, and on creating and strengthening neural pathways within and between modules in the brain.

The convergence in technology, evolution in digital resources and the demonstrable success of procedural approaches to learning offer huge opportunities to improve learning. Most of the education systems on earth are not geared up to take advantage of the opportunities yet, nor are most of the institutions within those systems. There are signs that the economic drivers for changing this situation are beginning to come into place.

Home is where the start is

The concept of education systems as in some ways separate from the rest of society has helped keep the focus on schools and universities. This is, of course, a misrepresentation: the home, peers and the wider society are the main influences on every person. It is beyond the scope of this book to look at the whole of society and its role in learning. Certainly all learners are affected by factors such as the economy, health services, environment, cultures and their immediate social contacts. Equally, all those factors are likely to be in a state of flux. Focusing on homes shows some of the interplay between these forces but also the significant shifts in the value of young people in homes (though this is relative progress, as children are probably the poorest, least powerful and most frequently abused age group – perhaps followed by the very elderly).

There are different responses to children's welfare, health and learning in different homes, and not all parents invest heavily in their children. At the moment a factor is that the poorest countries often have the highest birth rates and the richest the lowest. War does not seem a barrier to having many children – for example, in Afghanistan and Angola – and a lower birth rate can occur for no obvious reason, as in Estonia, where, with a seemingly brighter future after the end of its communist regime, the birth rate verges on being almost ten times lower. In general, the richer a country becomes the lower the birth rate, though there are exceptions. The situation in China demonstrates a slightly different trend: there has been a significant shift towards the importance of children as single-child families become more common (Hong Kong, for example, has one of the lowest birth rates in the world). Globally the picture is clear: the birth rate falls as the economy prospers, and richer families invest more – as a proportion of their income – in their children. This is, in the long term, good news for young people.

The current situation for children is, of course, extremely variable. Children on arrival at school are already unequal because of their country, carers and class. There exists a real opportunity to improve children's lives by finding successful ways of supporting children in homes, both to reduce extreme problems (such as malnutrition or obesity and other long-term health issues) and to impact positively on their learning. The cost effectiveness of such inventions could be justified by factoring in the considerable long-term health or productivity costs of not taking action. The idea that education and learning can rescue young people from their social and economic disadvantage without such interventions is simply a myth: in all countries, the rich have better educational outcomes. Learning is not a magic wand that can, on its own, produce social justice or right the wrongs of an economic system that punishes the young for the failures of their parents, community and society.

One of the main conclusions from good-quality international research is that where you live, and what your income and class are, matter to your education. Education outcomes matter to your economic outcomes. This does not just mean access to primary education (a key UN goal), but access to higher skills, or an advanced curriculum. Many children are denied access to higher-level learning experiences by segregation, gender, wealth, previous performance and other factors, including bias in teachers themselves. There are very few learning environments that are truly open for all children.

Home is where children start, and the differences between homes as places of learning are universally acknowledged. There has been a great deal done to attempt to address inequalities for children arising in part from inequalities in homes by using education systems to redress the balance (arguably, universal entitlement to education is one of those). Directly addressing inequalities in homes is less common: the Sure Start Programme in the US and UK, educational children's television, the kibbutz movement in Israel and other experiments suggest that direct intervention in homes and with parents can have positive outcomes. Recently reality shows in parental education focusing on poor parenting that can impact on health and emotional development may indicate the potential for alternative approaches to improving parental skills. 'Parenting classes' as a legal sanction for parents with challenging children and education in parenting for children in schools are other, more indirect, approaches. The political will to directly invest in homes and parents – for the sake of the children – is less evident, though disadvantaged community interventions and health initiatives are common in some countries. Again, there are justifications for high expenditure based on the costs of not intervening: taking children into the care of the state is very expensive and, globally, relatively rare, partly because such action historically has been littered with child abuse cases. Even Barnardo's, a very large UK children's charity that has done a lot to improve homes and families' lives, once shipped British children off to homes in Canada and other countries with wholly predictable negative consequences. On the other hand, the idea that formal education is an equitable and effective solution for young people growing up in poverty, poor environments, health problems and social disadvantage is naïve. Maximizing their learning and economic outcomes will mean tackling these more intractable issues directly, a task no government seems willing to undertake.

Yet there is a willingness in many parents to invest in learning and children. Guides for parents on child development, learning toys and child care are growing at an exponential rate. Parents are also beginning to see that active support of their children's learning is valuable far beyond the first few years, and some have taken over the responsibility entirely until university level. There are good economic reasons for this, one of which is the falling birth rate in many countries where growing disposable incomes are rising. This means that the investment in each child is seen as more important in terms of the financial value of the investment:

> More Koreans are sacrificing their financial planning for retirement in exchange for higher education, the Korea Institute of Finance (KIF) said Monday . . . the educational cost burden of Korean households accounted for 11 percent of monthly Korean household income last year, up from 6 percent in the early 1990s . . . the main reason behind the recent hike in educational spending is that the net return on educational investment is much greater than that from investment in other financial assets . . . with Korean adults preferring to have a late marriage, married Korean couples will opt to have less children and naturally they will put a greater educational expenditure on each child.
>
> (*Korean Times*: 7 March 2006)

The trends in countries with high investment in human resources generally may indicate the long-term trend to increased investment by parents in their

Figure 5.1 Older children teaching technology to families
Source: Family eLearning, Monkseaton, courtesy of North News

children. These trends have parallels in industry, with significant growth in expenditure in developing the skills and maximizing the potential of the workforce. High investment in people inevitably raises issues of the quality and value of the investment, but the movement towards improving learning for young people has begun – in part through the economic forces on families – and in the long term this will have positive outcomes. The process is, in effect, creating a market for better learning solutions, focused on what learners need to improve their potential earnings.

Learning without prejudice

Education systems have a very two-dimensional approach to learning where declarative learning and assessment are dominant. There is good research to indicate how learning can be delivered more effectively. In order to make real progress the world view about learning has to change to a scientific one.

The basic scientific starting point comprises two questions, 'What are the best ways to learn?' and 'What are the best learning outcomes?', and the simple answer to both questions is that no one knows exactly. The scientific process will use experiment to move closer to the answers, looking at all aspects of learning. There have to be measures of the impact of buildings, books and other resources, learning methods, and the actions of all people supporting learning (including parents). Severely critical tests have to be applied to national curricula and local curricula to see if they are valid or useful. Measurement of different kinds of outcomes for learners is necessary: their confidence; their knowledge and their skills with that knowledge; their understanding as well as their rote memory; and the long-term outcomes, such as whether they become independent, motivated learners. The fundamental change will be constantly relating the outcomes from neuroscientific research to rigorous social science outcomes, looking to link neuroscientific research on the brain to its practical application in learning (linking basic science with medical practice is a similar process).

Analysis of learning on so many different levels is a huge challenge, and the short-term outcomes may be hard to interpret, for example: 'Expectations of personal success correlate with persistent effort . . . [improvements could come with] discouraging competitive classroom contexts and encouraging positive interpersonal relationships.' Children who think they will be successful are also children who work persistently – the two go together, or correlate. The trouble is it is not clear if one causes the other, and if so, which one. Do hard workers think they are going to succeed because they work hard, or do children work hard because they believe they will succeed?. The research focus in social science studies can distort our understanding of learning during the process of establishing a scientific understanding. For example, the same study identified the different approaches researchers tended to take with different-aged children:

> [it appears] researchers have differing priorities in relation to type of 'learning behaviour' and different phases of education: that is, pre-school (social developmental); primary (cognitive development/learning); secondary (personal development and responsibility involving emotional, social and cognitive development); and that these differing priorities are associated with the selection of different theoretical explanations.
>
> (EPPI, Powell *et al.*: 11)

The underlying problem here is that researchers in their investigations reflect the nature of the education system itself – and its staff.

There is, nevertheless, huge potential to find new solutions and change learning for the better. Using rigorous social science methods we will find better ways of learning, better resources, better support for homes and better buildings, thus establishing a process of continuous improvement. All of this – however valuable as a starting point – is not enough on its own. Matching learning with the operations of the brain is the key to fundamental improvement. Innovations using different approaches to learning such as procedural, intuitive, emotional and even higher-order or ethical analysis are likely to have immediate benefits. If we are able to discover our mistakes in education, we still have to make appropriate changes. In the very short term, education has to learn the lessons such as those about grammar and violence in children – it must accept refutations – and stop making mistakes. In the long term, there will be a technological, economic and scientific convergence that revolutionizes learning.

Chapter 6

Education as politics

Abraham Lincoln and his son Tad in the 1860s

Source: NARA

Figure 6.1 March for jobs, about 100 years later
Source: NARA 1963

Politicians control the means of educational production

It may strike some as odd to describe education as a government industry where politicians control the means of production, but doing so highlights fundamental realities. Most children are educated in systems directly supported by taxation. These systems are controlled by government, and children are seen in policy terms as future employees and citizens of the country. In most countries the government is held accountable for education outcomes. This leads to a policy perspective stressing continuity and concentrating on educational outputs (often qualifications) in relation to education inputs (money).

The political control of education explains why ideological issues loom so large in education systems. For example, many education systems are formally secular (such as in the US and France) or religious (England and Iran). Politicians can favour systems based on selection by ability or religion, or they can encourage fee-paying schools; they can espouse particular teaching methods, or even punishments. The tendency for localization of education varies, from very local control (US), to nationalization with variations in kinds of schools (England and Japan), regionalization (Germany and Australia) and other variants – none of which is associated with improvements in children's learning. Despite their lack of expertise, politicians focus on the education system and stamp their prejudices (or those of the swing voters) onto it. Educational methods can also have political implications. For example, the use of a language in education can be enforced: in Wales all children must learn Welsh now that the Welsh education system has been freed from direct control from London; Franco's government in Spain forbade the teaching – or use – of Catalan in favour of Spanish; and in California and Texas there have been years of controversy about teaching in Spanish, in English or in both. In China, Mandarin has been the official language of China and education, though Cantonese is one of the world's most spoken languages. This linguistic politics has not died out, even in countries with multilingual populations:

> The mayor of Merchtem in Belgium has defended a ban on speaking French in the town's schools. Eddie de Block said the ban, introduced on Monday, would help all non-Dutch speakers integrate in the Flemish town near Brussels. Mr de Block insisted that the new measure did not violate human rights. Belgium has witnessed a number of language rows between the Dutch-speaking Flemish population and the French-speaking Walloons. 'It's not a great problem,' he said, adding that only about 8% of some 1,400 pupils in the town's four schools spoke languages other than Dutch.
>
> The ban means parents and children will only be allowed to speak Dutch on the school premises.
>
> Anyone caught speaking anything other than Dutch will be reprimanded by teachers.
>
> (BBC News Online: 1 September 2006)

The influx of French-speaking commuters into the town from nearby Brussels – or Bruxelles – is probably the cause of this ban. The aptly named Eddie de Block has demonstrated politicians' uncanny ability to make fools of themselves, in this case at the expense of children in a minority group.

Governments and their policy advisors pursue their own agenda through education. Political self-interest, and the self-interest of policy advisors, should not be underestimated as a shaping force in education systems. There are other pressures on government to see education as another political process: because most educational funding comes from government, officials' discussions with educationalists are accompanied – directly or indirectly – by requests for additional funding. The tension between political imperatives and educational self-interest does not create an ideal environment for the improvement of children's learning. Too often political and funding pressures result in failed visions, research and policy. There are even incentives to fail or to educate slowly: for example, if a child is held back to redo a year schools can gain an extra year's funding; US universities take four years when most European universities take three, and so collect another year's fees; or extra funding is given for every child with learning difficulties, which rewards the labelling of more children as having learning difficulties and discourages help to overcome them. More widely education systems, like nations, more often see themselves in competition with each other, rather than in cooperation. The educational world, like the political world, might best be characterized as an intellectual, cultural and organizational ghetto.

Children and parents have almost no input into educational policy, choice of schools or funding for education. They are caught up in the bureaucratic process of the education on offer where they live. It has been argued that parents could, if they chose, be more successful in creating learning systems at home, but that is no more a solution than the current situation of every country creating its own education system. The outcome of our politicized education processes is that education has become a multi-billion dollar and largely unaccountable bureaucratic government industry. Throughout the world people labour to re-invent the wheel while under the direct control of politicians, working largely within educational silos.

Why government policies don't work

Government is not a simple process, and education policy is as prone to problems as any other government activity. Governments tend to work within departments (for example, the Department of Education in the US or Japan's equivalent, Monbusho). The people in these departments are rarely experienced educationalists or researchers, and often not even experts in education. The development of government policy reflects this. Policy units, the origin of many changes in education systems, are staffed with people who are very unlikely to represent the best thinking about education – as full-time government employees they often move from department to department, or slowly crawl up the government or political employment ladder. For policy advisors, or permanent government officials, the conventional wisdom, with its widely accepted judgements, is ideal. Anything else is a risk and the public sector is very risk averse. To be fair, some in government are aware of the limitations of their approach. They talk in private about the need for changes, but these are rarely implemented: the process they use is slow and intended to be safe (safe from blame, that is, not safe for learners in the current education system). There are organizational issues too: the coordination between different units in the UK's Department for Education and Skills (DfES) means senior officials attend so many meetings that, at times, not one person is present in a meeting from beginning to end.

Those deciding education policy can be products of fee-paying schools, and some do not even use the services they direct. Often their vision of education is out of date and out of touch. I remember speaking to a very senior official in the UK's education department about languages. He suggested to me that Latin was the ideal choice for a £1 million investment of public money in a digital learning system. I argued (as, no doubt, many others did) that the demand for Latin in the world at large – and in business – lagged somewhat behind the demand for Spanish, German and French (and, indeed, almost any other modern language). His argument was that Latin was the bedrock of good education (perhaps the education that he felt he had experienced some 30 years earlier), and that children across the country would benefit. It was a rather quaint approach, but one with unfortunate consequences. The money went on Latin. Of course politicians, who are responsible for controlling officials and long-term government employees, come and go. These politicians usually have little experience in education. In 2006 the US Secretary of State was Margaret Spellings (whose experience was confined to policy and political work) and in the UK the Secretary of State for Education and Skills was Ruth Kelly (with no direct experience at all), and they are typical of politicians who control education systems, and who respond to the advice of their officials.

Even educational outcomes are subject to government and education establishment whim. Qualifications are usually created by bodies closely allied to government, and are country or even locality specific. These qualifications are created by committees, members of the education establishment who embed in qualifications what they were taught or what they see as in the long-term interests of their subject. A depressing example of this is the obsession with Shakespeare in England, where students have formal, national examinations at 14 (featuring a Shakespeare play), 16 (requiring a Shakespeare play) and 18 (which can feature more than one Shakespeare play). This can also lead to a very limited experience in other areas: a child needs to be familiar with fewer than 28 poems to tackle the formal English Literature examination at 16. Changing these qualifications slightly is, however, a useful method of deflecting criticism of the government, so it's often used, creating organizational churn that can take years to settle down.

The people employed to develop policy in education, and the governments they serve, have clear incentives to achieve political outcomes. Quite naturally the processes they employ are focused on avoiding criticism and creating a short-term public impression of improvement. They are helped in this by the Hawthorne Effect. Hawthorne was a researcher in industry who examined the impact of changing factory methods. In a series of experiments, he discovered that almost any kind of reorganization or change improved production in the short term, though production would then rapidly return to previous levels. Educational initiatives work in this way, creating the short-term boost for politicians, thus creating an incentive to use them – and then to move quickly on before they begin to fail. Those managing education systems are then left with the problem of quietly burying the initiative. These contrasts between the interests of the government and its employees on the one hand, and the interests of the governed, and those in education, on the other, are the root of the negative impact of politics on education. Education systems as they currently operate are not good enough for our children, but the control of change lies in the hands of those who do not have the knowledge, skills or incentives necessary to change them for the better. Not surprisingly they fail to meet the aspirations of children, parents and society.

Education systems are political

Learners are presented with an image of the world shaped by different political, geographic, ideological and cultural prejudices. Political control of education systems can be even more overt at times, impacting directly on the people involved. For example, all married women teachers in Colorado during the Depression were fired, as the state legislators felt they were taking jobs from men and depriving other families of an income. For women teachers who were the only employed family member, it meant they had to leave the state – and many did. The impact of politics also touches leaders of prestigious institutions. Clark Kerr, President of the University of California at Berkeley, was fired for being too left wing, along with other employees, through the secret activities of Californian politicians linked with the Federal Bureau of Investigation (FBI) (including Ronald Reagan, later to be US president). The notorious McCarthy anti-communist witch-hunts in the 1950s had affected many in Hollywood, but this interference in California's education system was kept secret until recently. The extent of the political cleansing of the US education system even meant that Einstein was covertly pursued by the FBI while a professor in US universities. These cases of individual abuses pale into insignificance in comparison with larger political changes. The cultural revolution in China saw many higher education institutions completely altered, with many staff sent to work on farms, and there were radically changed educational experiences for children throughout the country. European communist education systems were transformed in the post-glasnost era, though the degree of change varied considerably from country to country. Perhaps the education system in South Africa pre- and post-apartheid shows one of most radical shifts of all, where racial, financial, curricular, political and institutional upheavals were absolute. The success the country has had in overcoming these problems is limited in some areas, but progress has been impressive in others: in the university sector there has been successful partnering between higher education establishments formerly either all black or all white in South Africa's different regions. These upheavals show the impact a government can have on an education system should it choose to.

Political control can also routinely influence what is taught in education. The largely hidden battle between governments and pressure groups over what is taught is probably seen most often in religion and history. As history is seen as forming political views it is frequently an area of open debate:

> [the UK's Qualifications and Curriculum Authority called for reform] but critics on the left and right want to push the process further and faster. On the right, there is an appetite for more patriotic history. But the left is also keen to reclaim a different version of Britishness . . .
>
> (*The Guardian*: 3 January 2005)

History is one of the few areas – other than religion – that cause countries to openly disagree on educational matters. Japan became embroiled in real controversy in 2005 with Korea and China. The main problems arose because of a conflict about the Imperial Army's war crimes in the Second World War (never a popular subject in Japanese political life):

> Tokyo's public school board has adopted a new edition of a Japanese history textbook that has provoked protests in China and South Korea. The book, criticised for distorting Japan's militarist past, will be used . . . to teach children for four years, starting next year. The move could re-ignite a diplomatic dispute which first flared when the government approved the book in April.
>
> (BBC News Online: 28 July 2005)

The textbook was originally approved by the Tokyo school board for a few schools, with references to these crimes omitted, and the controversy grew as other school boards followed suit. Korea and China both formally complained about the omissions. This controversy was unusual because it focused international attention on the different interpretation of history and also because it involved countries exerting political pressure to change textbooks in a neighbouring education system.

Political control even extends to how children are taught, not just on large issues – such as selection in schools, ages of transfer, the curriculum, policy and so on – but even down to issues such as which methods should be used to teach. Reading and mathematics are common targets for political directives, often in response to media panics or critical reports. In England in the late 1990s both reading and mathematics in the primary sector were targets at the same time when both a national literacy strategy and a national numeracy strategy were published. These strategies involved directing all the teachers in the country how to teach, down to the length of time for certain activities in each lesson. From time to time new subjects or approaches are also created and placed in the curriculum because of demands from society, or the whim of government. The most common recent example worldwide is ICT. The results can be less than ideal, as the teachers, resources and methods of teaching often need to be improvised, entirely free of any strong evidence about how the innovation should be delivered. In the case of ICT a fundamental question was whether it should be used as a tool for learning, or as a new subject. For example, in a secondary school in Hiroshima in the early 1990s I was proudly shown a typical classroom jammed with state-of-the-art PCs with enormous screens (and very little room for students). The 40 students were all doing exactly the same thing, key stroke by key stroke, under the rigid direction of the teacher. At the other extreme, I recently walked around a new school building in England, equipped with an electronic white-board in every classroom. Only one was in use, showing a popular commercial film.

Education is a politicized activity in its aims, structures and methods, and all of this diverts attention from learning. Education policy has broadly failed to deliver big improvements in education and, like many other government controlled activities, has not yet shown the rapid improvement seen in technology and science. At times, education policy initiatives descend into bad politics: they create or respond only to media panics, intense lobbying or pressures from institutions, and they see the direct political use of educational issues for electoral or other party advantage as a key aspect of education and education systems.

Is more better?

The image of education systems as an industry helps explain how governments approach learning. Education is a process to improve the potential of the human resource in economic terms and the adjustment of citizens to the kind of government they have in political terms. The education industry – the institutions that deliver education – has been quite successful in convincing society that its systems and qualifications are necessary to produce the products – educated workers – that society needs. The industry has incentives to create new pathways and learning programmes that extend the time and money spent on education, arguing that these will improve the economy and society. Years spent in education is a measure of quantity (how long) rather than quality (how effective), and it has tended to dominate government and international debate on educational inequality:

> During the 1990s primary education enrolments increased in every region, and in many a large proportion of children are enrolled. In East Asia and the Pacific, Central and Eastern Europe and the Commonwealth of Independent States (CIS) and Latin America and the Caribbean more than 90% of children are enrolled in primary school. In South Asia 79% are enrolled, and in the Arab States 77%. In Sub-Saharan Africa net primary enrolments increased by 3 percentage points in the 1990s, yet less than 60% of children are enrolled.
>
> (UN Development Programme: 92)

The global picture is one of improving access to education for the poorest, but with hidden problems that limit the real economic benefit:

> Of the 680 million children of primary school age in developing countries, 115 million do not attend school – three-fifths of them girls. In India 40 million children are not in primary school, more than a third of the world's total. Moreover, enrolment does not mean completion. Just over half the children who start primary school finish it – and in Sub-Saharan Africa, just one in three. Reflecting these shortcomings, one-quarter of adults in the developing world cannot read or write.
>
> (UN Development Programme: 92)

It is legitimate to consider access to primary education an important indicator that standards of education are improving globally, and to see literacy as a key target and as a skill that allows access to many forms of post-school learning. Globally, 100 years ago those who could read were in the minority, and now they are in the majority. This is progress, as more people have access to education systems and to essential life skills such as reading and writing. Taking a long-term, global view, there has been real progress, though the cost has been substantial.

More sophisticated measures of human development suggest that, although access to education is improving, there remain enormous disparities between countries, and within countries. The UN's Education Measure shows this (see Table 6.1). Scores near 1 indicate very high educational attainment by the population, and scores of about 0.75 the average educational attainment. Although it is not a precise measure by any means, it does reflect a general picture that is probably broadly correct.

In terms of access to education, the broad conclusion is that rich people and societies can afford more education than poorer people and societies – and this is no surprise. The overall strength of the economy matters, so poor children in wealthy countries do better than poor children in poor countries. People in advanced economies do better than those from less advanced economies. So, on the level of individual wealth, country wealth and country development, those classed as 'haves' do better than the 'have nots'. From the point of view of children, access to learning appears to be restricted by where they live and how much money their family has. The underlying assumption of the UN in all its educational documents is one that is common in government: more education is, like gross national product, good: the more you have, the better it is.

Governments worldwide use increases in number of years spent in education and student numbers in higher education as a demonstration that their policies are working. The political debate often reverts to improving educational products in terms of sheer volume: more children have access to primary school (a central UN focus), more children have access to degrees (a current UK focus), more children achieve higher degrees (a focus in the US and China).

Table 6.1 United Nations Education Measure

United Nations Education Measure	Average
By region	
All developing countries	0.71
Least developed countries	0.49
Arab States	0.61
East Asia and the Pacific	0.83
Latin America and the Caribbean	0.86
South Asia	0.57
Sub-Saharan Africa	0.56
Central and Eastern Europe and the CIS	0.93
OECD countries	0.94
High-income OECD	0.97
By countries grouped by level of education	
High human development	0.95
Medium human development	0.75
Low human development	0.50
By income group	
High income	0.97
Middle income	0.84
Low income	0.59
World average	0.76

Notes: Education Measure: 1 is very high, 0.75 is about average. This is a composite measure based on available data, not based on actual tests of samples within each country, area or group.

Source: UN 2004: summary.

However, countries making exceptional progress in the level of qualifications are already considering the issue of quality and not just quantity:

> China and India . . . recognize the importance of technology and education in the competitive global marketplace . . . Asia today graduates more than three times the number of engineers and scientists than the United States does. The challenge is to improve the quality as they increase the quantity.
> (Stiglitz: 44)

The political opposition can then argue that the standards are slipping because, it is assumed, it is not possible for more people to participate at higher levels without the education standards at those levels being reduced. This almost universal approach by governments has the benefit of increasing access to higher levels of education to new cohorts of students – but there are inherent weaknesses in such an approach.

The relentless increase in the cost of education systems is, however, a problem. It is not politically easy to challenge the educational establishment, yet governments do try to achieve economies in light of the rise in real costs, for example by encouraging the use of fee paying in education or by attracting commercial funding. The rising cost of education is already impacting on families in most of the advanced economies where university education is paid for by the students or their families. In Korea (where it has now become a central family item of expenditure), the US, England and Australia, people are making university education a key financial priority, with universities now largely businesses in their approach. This market approach to education is linked with universities extending the average length of formal education. There are clear differences between universities, too: whereas Oxford and Cambridge award MA degrees to all students after three years, other universities require students to attend (and pay) for four or even five years for the same degree. The students have little choice: universities control the qualification process, and there are few alternative pathways to a degree other than attending a conventional university.

The fundamental problem with this approach to education as a product, where greater investment gives you a longer-to-produce but more valuable product, is that it is not sustainable. The longer it takes to educate a child, the shorter their working life. And changes in the economy from scientific and technological drivers mean that there are huge issues of knowledge redundancy during the educational process: what they learn can be out of date in only a few years in science and technology. The economy is seeking high levels of skills, which is an approach not always encouraged in education, and businesses are looking again at the quality of the education their recruits possess. Students and parents are beginning to look at quality, too, and are more frequently moving country for their education if they feel it will offer a better quality outcome.

At the moment in the education system concepts of efficiency, value for money, and the impact on children's working lives play little part. The unheard voices are those of children who face a very long commitment to a system and process that most do not believe in, yet holds real power over their lives and their future. Parents and employers also feel disenfranchized from an educational process that is not very responsive to their concerns. The public debates over education are not often about efficiency and appropriateness of degrees – yet. A key question is whether society has any good guide as to whether the political system is delivering an education system that is getting better.

The battle for minds: measures

Very few people think it is a well-known fact that education systems are improved by politicians who institute reforms (except politicians: 'School system improves under our bright light' – a letter to the editor of *The Wall Street Journal* on 5 April 2006 from US Secretary of State for Education

Margaret Spellings being a good example). These politicians are rather out-weighed by those who see reform as the normal state of education, citing examples such as: Japan's National Commission on Educational Reform set up in 2000, and its Rainbow Plan; China's similar process begun in 1987; New Zealand's Tertiary Reforms of 2006; and Australia's similar reforms in the 2003 Support Act. Waves of reforms in former communist countries in Europe are often radical in very limited respects, such as the ideological Polish reforms. The political rhetoric is often dramatic, but the changes in the system are often less extreme.

National assessment of an education system is clearly a two-edged sword for governments: they need positive assessment to show the government is doing well, but they need negative assessment to show reforms are necessary. Often governments have ongoing assessment of schools and educational practice, both qualitative and quantitative. Qualitative assessment is carried out, usually by former teachers, as in England's Office for Standards in Education (Ofsted) (previously Her Majesty's Inspectors of Schools). The inspectors go to schools, watch lessons and read materials, and decide whether the school is doing a good job. Quantitative approaches are usually about final assessment results on some kind of examination or assessment that is not at a recognizable international standard, for example in California:

> State law authorized the development of the *California High School Exit Examination* (*CAHSEE*), which students in California public schools must pass to earn a high school diploma beginning in the 2005–06 school year. The purpose of the *CAHSEE* is to . . . ensure that students who graduate from high school can demonstrate competency in reading, writing, and mathematics. (See www.cde.ca.gov for the CAHSEE saga.)

If we judge our educators through subjective evaluations carried out by former educators, we are almost certain to reinforce conventional wisdom – in effect, such methods are worse than useless. Assessments based on quantitative measures can be more useful, especially if other information is included in the analysis. It is very rare to find both methods used to analyse the same problem, but it does happen.

Government reforms are a factor in every education system, and it is often almost impossible to find good evidence about their impact. It is for this reason that one of the world's most revealing examinations of government reforms was conducted by the UK's National Audit Office. A key feature of this research was that it was not carried out by a governmental education agency: the National Audit Office's job is to assess value for money in all government spending. In order to evaluate the effect of reforms the National Audit Office examined the enormous amount of data government agencies already held about education in a rigorous social science model to see what government initiatives worked, and the effectiveness of the standards watchdog, England's Ofsted. Based on a huge statistical analysis of children, background factors and outcomes, the report's conclusions were stark: the conventional wisdom about education was wrong in almost every case.

Ofsted is meant both to judge school performance and to ensure that standards rise. The National Audit Office looked at schools that Ofsted identified as failing and carefully analysed the children's results, taking into account background factors. Almost all of the schools labelled failing by Ofsted were in the most challenging neighbourhoods, with the most challenging children. The result of the research? Some 80 per cent of the schools labelled failing by Ofsted were not failing at all, and 20 per cent were doing an excellent job. The report showed that Ofsted's judgements were worse than useless – the failing schools might just as well have been chosen at random.

Other findings from the National Audit Office's report were equally harsh, showing that few things coming from government made a real difference to children. No government reform, bar one, had produced improvements. Faith-based schools – encouraged by government – did not improve results; Education Action Zones were not effective; and performance-related pay had not made a significant difference. The evidence also demonstrated that conventional wisdom was wrong: sending a child to a grammar school (a selective school admitting only children who test highly for academic ability) would be likely to ensure they did less well in examinations at 16 compared to those in non-selective schools. The only government reform to work was the specialist schools initiative: children in specialist schools clearly outperformed those in non-specialist schools. Although the report did not explore the issue, this reform was actually linked to an incentive – extra money. To become a specialist school, the staff must raise £50,000 from industry, which is then matched by the government. The school then receives extra funding yearly – about 3 per cent of its total budget. If the schools results are not good, they lose their specialist status – and the funding. The lesson of this reform may be that financial incentives work if they are closely tied to delivering improved outcomes.

It would be logical in light of this research to reassess government reforms and Ofsted. Yet the recommendations from the National Audit Office's report were not taken forward. The media chose not to use it to challenge some persistent myths in education (ones the media often reinforce), and the government continued with reforms rather than incentives. Ofsted remains in place, judging schools in an antiquated, expensive and inaccurate way. Parents still cannot trust the information they get about how good schools are, or the impact of government reforms. The underlying message is disturbing: governments have the information needed to identify what is making a difference but they do not use it – they prefer the illusion of progress to the rigour of knowledge.

The battle for minds: the aims

Education systems aim to instil knowledge (broken up into locally defined subjects), local cultural values, nationalism and, possibly, a religion. There are no education systems that actively aim to instil children with religious freedom, international flexibility, ethical values they determine and an integrated view of knowledge. Education systems do not encourage independent, self-motivated learners: conformity and compliance are more valued attributes. At their worst, education systems can be repressive as well as regressive:

> In the Jamia Hafza Madrassa (religious school) in Pakistan's capital, Islamabad, hundreds of girls are taking their exams . . . but although they are taught subjects like maths and geography, they are not tested on them. Their exams are only on matters relating to Islam.
>
> (BBC News Online: 19 September 2005)

Nor is religious indoctrination just an issue in the Muslim world in openly religious systems – in the United States the same tensions exist even in an openly secular system:

> US scientists have called on mainstream religious communities to help them fight policies that undermine the teaching of evolution. The American Association for the Advancement of Science (AAAS) hit out at the 'intelligent design' movement . . . There have been several attempts across the US by anti-evolutionists to get intelligent design taught in school science lessons . . . Last year, a federal judge ruled in favour of 11 parents in Dover, Pennsylvania, who argued that Darwinian evolution must be taught as fact. Dover school administrators had pushed for intelligent design to be inserted into science teaching. But the judge ruled this violated the constitution, which sets out a clear separation between religion and state. Despite the ruling, more challenges are on the way.
>
> (BBC News Online: 20 February 2006)

The debate here is about the nature of scientific knowledge, but also about the inculcation of a particular, local religious world view as part of the education of all local children. The growing diversity in local communities throughout the world as globalization accelerates makes this imposition of a religious world view even less acceptable.

The current agenda for education systems is governmental, economic and institutional: the purpose seems to be to create children as products to fit into the current society. Educational change seems to arise from temporary political necessity, internal bureaucratic infighting, or as a knee-jerk response to a media panic. Parents are aware that their children's education can be a bit of a lottery. They know that it depends on where they live, on their income and on the teachers their children have. Too often a child's progress depends on finding that elusive motivating teacher, or book or television series. Good parents and employers know children need to be independent, enthusiastic learners with good interpersonal skills, but still tolerate educational qualifications and judgements that do not show these skills and qualities. Parents are aware of the educational treadmill that seems to stretch forward into their child's early adulthood, and feel they are trapped by the system.

What we have today is an education system built on ignorance. The irony of a system created to educate everyone that does not even know how children learn is obvious, but tragic. Education systems' shortcomings are not necessarily the fault of teachers. There is nothing wrong with our children, yet many fail to do well. A large part of the failure is the fault of the systems, methods and control of education. Fundamentally, the problem is that the aims of current systems are wrong in practice: we force children to spend much of their childhood in education institutions so they can be judged and categorized; their day-to-day experience in education is often poor; and what they learn is, at its worst, simply local beliefs and, more often, simply useless.

Chapter 7

Free learning

We may live locally, but increasingly we will have to think globally, think
of ourselves as part of a global community.

(Joseph Stiglitz, *Making Globalization Work*)

Learning is a right

Learning is a biological necessity, like eating: people are constantly interacting
with the environment and developing responses to it. Education is different:
it was created to transfer a limited range of knowledge between generations

Source: courtesy of North News

and tends to use a limited range of methods. It has been argued that child care, the opportunity for the state to inculcate social and political values, and encouraging conformity are as important as learning in schools and universities. This judgement may be harsh, but it does reflect some education systems' faults.

On the other hand, if children are seen as citizens – rather than a different legal caste to be moulded to society's purposes – then they are entitled to 'life, liberty and the pursuit of happiness', to learning that gives intellectual freedom, respects children's religious and cultural liberties and develops their adaptive skills to all societies: children can aim to be independent, self-motivated learners. This has not, as yet, featured largely in education – or even in educational research:

> None [of these studies] has examined teacher effectiveness on independent learning . . . which encourages and enables students to learn for themselves, to develop metacognitive awareness, to take some control over the learning process by being less dependent on the teacher and more ready to challenge the received wisdom.
>
> (Campbell *et al.*: 119)

Young people should be supported in these goals. There is a need to re-shape how they learn: learning should be more about processes and skills than facts, more about curiosity than intellectual conformity – and global, not local.

Learning content, processes and aims need radical renewal, and solutions lie in looking at learning as a process, not a set of static information. At the same time a major societal effort is required to establish the scientific understanding of learning. The changing nature of the environment is another fundamental consideration: the impact of science and technologies alters not just our environment but the skills people need to adapt successfully within it. Finally, older people are themselves limited by their learning experiences. Advances in learning face a generational gap: the impact of older people and conventional society on young people who learn in a different way will not always be positive. Nor do our industrial, environmental, political and social structures necessarily foster learning in children, young people or adults.

The scale of the challenge to change education systems extends beyond the formal system and the people who interact with it. The importance of other environments on learning is now firmly established in rigorous research: the physical environment (such as housing or the immediate area); the learner's economic circumstances; the social context; and other factors. Money is the key: 93 per cent of children in India do not proceed beyond primary education, and many of those do not complete even that stage. On the other hand, hardly any of the top 5 per cent of the world's wealthiest families have children who do not attend higher education. In work the same inequalities exist: many organizations fail to train staff or support lifelong learning – this most commonly affects people in poorly paid jobs. Those in highly paid employment are expected and encouraged to continue learning.

There are more individual influences: parents can be a negative influence for an individual child of any background. Poor parents can have histories of emotional, social, educational or other disadvantages, and the problems they cause for children cannot, at the moment, be overcome easily, even later in life. A good physical environment, good health and freedom from violence all contribute to learning, and for many children these are only aspirations. Improving learning for people should be a major undertaking for society, not unlike that of improving – and preserving – health. Indeed, they are related: both focus on meeting fundamental human needs that are, by their very nature, extremely complex. This does not, however, prevent radical improvements in well-being: medicine is, of course, much further advanced than learning at the moment, but it is likely that the two will eventually merge on some levels, as in neuroscience. A scientific understanding of learning and health will end the current abuse of drugs in learning contexts, such as the increasing use of dangerous drugs to alter behaviour in de-motivating classrooms:

> Already there are reports of an alarming increase in the use of prescribed drugs medicating the classroom, whether it be Ritalin for enhancing concentration, Prozac for enhancing mood, or Pro-vigil for extending alert wakefulness. The problems with these drugs is that they do not target a single trait . . . partly because . . . drugs manipulate, in a very broad way, the chemicals in the brain. And that, in turn, could have widespread and long-lasting effects.
>
> (Susan Greenfield, Professor of Pharmacology, Oxford:
> *The Guardian*: 25 April 2006)

Learning and health are intertwined, and both contribute to our sense of well-being: crude pharmacological interventions will not improve learning. Better solutions will be created by approaching learning from a completely different perspective.

The wind of change

The importance of overcoming the limitations created by current education systems is fuelled by many factors: the economic necessity of higher skills, financing education for ever longer periods of time, advances in social science methodology and comparisons with the huge advances in science, technology and medicine. Calls for improvements in educational outcomes are important political issues not just in a few countries but in South Africa, Japan, China, the US, the UK, OECD countries, the European Union, Malaysia, Australia and New Zealand. For populations under economic pressure, such as the

Palestinians, educational success has become even more important. There are also treasury pressures to improve value for money in education, or to shift the burden of funding education onto families. This need to radically improve education is, however, different from the traditional complaint that 'things aren't what they used to be': calling for the good old days is hollow when one of the needs is for ICT professionals.

Governments and society are now more accustomed to seeking scientific-style solutions to social policy issues, though it has long been recognized as a way of improving society, even in Elizabethan times. A century ago the hope of a scientific breakthrough in education was high. Researchers hoped an application of social science methods, including experiment, could reveal effective teaching: 'These conceptions of effective teaching were innovative for their time in that they were based on experimentation, demonstration and observation, and were thus research-based.' These attempts failed to change education because the complexity of the task was greater than the capacity of the social science methods available at that time. Now there is even some attention on educational improvement through a wider view of the child, such as the UK's *Every Child Matters* policy, where economic, health and educational goals are, at least, linked. These changes are the exception: more often, educational accountability means outcomes, as in the supposedly scientific measures of educational outcomes in US states and in South-east Asia's rigid expectations of children's progress. The move towards a more rigorous approach is, in the end, unstoppable because of the incentive to improve. Learning is now seen as too important to be left to education systems, and training as too valuable to be ignored in business because human resources are fundamental to economic power. The globalized reporting on education performance creates league tables based on a common measure of learning, and show some countries are making rapid progress and others are not – and this rank order in learning progress is also true of their economic performance. The economic message is clear: good learning is good for business. Suddenly child care, indoctrination and conformity seem less important.

Globalized business is already taking advantage of the cheaper educated personnel available outside its traditional recruitment areas, creating concerns about the future in countries such as the US:

> As each generation of public leaders takes office, it must ask how its stewardship will be remembered. Will it be recalled because, on its watch, the administration, Congress, and OERI [Office of Educational Research and Improvement] stood by as the nation's schools continued to fall short of their potential? . . . Will they wonder why this generation of leaders refused to take advantage of the most powerful tool at its disposal for improving student achievement, research and the generation of new knowledge? [Or] . . . It can live in honored memory because it insisted

that education is the key to the American future. Scholars can document how it put forward a new vision of what education could be in the United States. And citizens may forever be grateful because these leaders helped rally the nation behind this promising new image and joined hands with the research community to make this vision a reality.

(NERPPB: 11–12)

The rhetoric seems simplistic and the solution self-serving, but the concern was real. As pressure of this kind mounted, the US government responded with the *No Child Left Behind Act* of 2002, which called for a more rigorous assessment of education as a requirement, not an option. The government response was, in part, driven by an electoral concern: the desperation of American parents who were – perhaps intuitively – realizing the futility of relying on getting children into seemingly good schools and other means of ensuring their success in learning. This intuition was demonstrated by the lottery system devised in Chicago to determine the allocation of school places. Parents had their requests for schools put into a lottery, and the children were allocated by chance to local schools. Later, the results of those children were examined to see whether children who got their parents' choice of school did better: the results demonstrated something quite different from what the parents might originally have imagined:

> The result is a natural experiment on a grand scale. This was hardly the goal in the mind of the Chicago school officials who conceived the lottery. But when viewed in this way, the lottery offers a wonderful means of measuring just how much school choice – or, really, a better school – truly matters.
>
> So what do the data reveal?
>
> The answer will not be heartening to obsessive parents: in this case, student choice barely mattered at all.
>
> (*Freakonomics*: 158)

Of course American parents are not alone in their concerns: as parents become richer, and the number of children they have fewer – a common feature of industrialized societies – their focus on ensuring economic advantage for their children increases.

Under pressure from international competition, financial pressure and citizen dissatisfaction with the slow progress of education, the success story of medicine over the last 200 years might seem very attractive from behind the barricades in departments of education beginning to fear that endless reforms will not, in the end, be enough to prevent them from facing the political consequences of educational failure. This political awakening is good news for future generations, but the answers will not be found through political means.

Can government trust schools?

The reform of education by politicians has a long history, littered with initiatives. Some of these initiatives are aimed at breaking down barriers in education and society. For example, the European Commission's research and development programmes all require institutions from different countries to work together, usually as a partnership between universities and the private sector. Recently there has been a move to link schools with business in the hope that this will lead to improvements in schools, especially in the US and UK. The specialist schools movement in the UK offered matched funding to schools that partnered with business to establish a specialism in a subject, but the outcomes seem to indicate that the incentive of the long-term additional funding (for better outcomes) was the key to improvement. Often the partnership with business was quickly dropped once the additional funding was achieved.

More recently Academies and Trust schools have been created in the UK, where significant long-term partnerships between schools and business have been made, as an alternative to the control of schools by local government. The reaction against these initiatives was fierce, especially from the education establishment, and the Labour government was only able to pass the legislation with the support of the Conservative party. Opposition to the new approach came from senior figures, including former Labour leader Neil Kinnock and former Secretary of State for Education Estelle Morris. The debate was very heated indeed, and alternative proposals were put forward that tried to ensure local government control of schools, as well as ensuring no increase in selection in these new schools. The scale of the parliamentary rebellion – Labour MPs voted against their own government – was one of the largest the then Prime Minister, Tony Blair, ever faced. The Trust schools were, some believed, modelled on Victorian philanthropic or religious trusts, where benefactors created schools and other public services in deprived areas in major cities (perhaps because the Trusts were to be charities). Others saw the Trusts as a method of separating the responsibility of running schools from local government control, and freeing schools from bureaucracy – and freeing politicians from blame for their shortcomings.

Tony Blair, at a meeting in 10 Downing Street just before the legislation was voted on in parliament, offered a different argument. He said that government did not have all the answers to improving schools and, like other public services, it was necessary to create mechanisms for bottom-up reform and not just centralized reform. He believed major advances had been made in school education, but reform needed to continue. Blair felt that the Trust approach was one that would free schools, foster innovation and spread improvements across the system. It is interesting that the Prime Minister, after almost two decades of centralization in English education – starting with his predecessor Margaret Thatcher – was turning to deregulation as a partial solution to improving schools. The more cynical observers saw this approach offering powerful pressure groups – such as religious groups, certain sectors of industry and fee-paying schools – an opportunity to take over state education.

The response of the business community during the controversy was remarkably muted, with the exception of a few, such as Microsoft Education who – in a partnership with Monkseaton High School and the Open University – had been suggesting to the DfES for some time that open and distance learning and new technologies could make a contribution to improving education in all schools. This partnership suggested that an Academy be created based on distance learning, supporting those not in school. This proposal was rejected in the form of an Academy, but shortly before the White Paper that announced the new Trust school legislation was published in October 2005, Andrew Adonis – often considered as the policy lead behind the proposals – wrote to me:

> It seems to me that the necessary elements are in place at Monkseaton to develop the project as a pathfinder and exemplar of what we hope to achieve across the system. If you and your partners agree, we would very much like to include your plans in the announcement [of the White Paper] . . . This is a very exciting project and you will be a national trailblazer!
>
> (Andrew Adonis: 18 October 2005)

When the original proposals of the partnership between Microsoft, Monkseaton and the Open University are examined, is seems clear that Tony Blair's account of the purpose of Trust schools is almost identical to Andrew Adonis's. So what exactly did this partnership offer that made it a possible 'exemplar of what we hope to achieve across the system'? The original proposal was ambitious:

> The Academy will be [a base for distance and online learning] creating new ways of learning and teaching that personalise education for students wherever they are, whatever school they attend. It will offer special support for students who have difficulties accessing education: the ill, those with disabilities, those in care, and those temporarily abroad.
>
> (Partnership Briefing for DfES)

The use of the experience of the Open University and the software of Microsoft to create educational experiences for students in – and out – of schools makes sense: scaleable solutions for learning are – as both organizations have demonstrated – perfectly possible now. The nature of the innovation is clear, building upon the success of the Open University in higher education by transferring its techniques to the school sector to meet learner needs.

The project evolved within the Trust framework and acquired the label 'innovation trust'. The principles of all the parties involved were made clear early on: to have fair (non-selective) access to Monkseaton High School for local children, to develop better solutions for learners and schools, to share those innovations across the system, and not to take a partisan, religious or ideological stance in relation to learning. The Open University found it could not be a formal partner in a Trust school, though it agreed to work closely with the partnership through different means. The cooperation of the world's largest company and Europe's largest university with an ordinary high school in a neglected region of England was ideal from the government's point of view as it showed that the Trust school arrangements were not necessarily elitist. The focus on open and distance learning meant that many of the innovations planned by the Trust could be easily shared as well.

Most of the innovations were to do with the learning environment: creating a flexible, personal digital learning environment, creating a new school building that radically changed the physical environment for learning, offering degree courses to younger students and full degrees starting at 16, and sharing innovation, such as supporting modern languages in thousands of other schools. It was argued that this approach to innovation in a range of areas, if replicated in many schools and rigorously evaluated, could be a powerful engine for change. However, the Trust mechanism could, as others foresaw, still be used for many different approaches, including the control of schools by religious organizations or private school trusts.

The approach of deregulating the relationships between schools and other organizations lies at the heart of the Trust school approach, and the attempt was probably driven by thoughts that leadership would be improved through business input and that – possibly – greater resources might come into schools. The long-term picture is less clear: there is no necessary connection between the government deregulating aspects of education and improvements in learning – though it may make some forms of innovation easier. Trust and Academy schools might prove a powerful tool for improving education – and might not. In principle, deregulation is fundamentally limited: allowing many people to go down different paths does not necessarily mean they will discover better solutions that will then spread across the education system.

What is missing is the recognition that improving learning needs to work through a new scientific process. Removing a layer of bureaucratic legal constraints created to organize and direct schools is useful, but not system-changing. Education law – like law in general – is, in effect, a collection of conventional wisdom: it has a deadening effect on a dynamic society's learning. Removing the restraints en masse might not work either, but the government's approach is, as often occurs in education, essentially piecemeal. The basic legal controls on schools remain, even if the restrictions have become shared between the Department for Education and Skills and the Charity Commission. It may be that better models of learning are created with this small set of new freedoms, but there is no reason to assume that will happen. In effect, there is not a solution to the regulation by politicians that the politicians can implement by changing small aspects of the law. Solutions lie elsewhere.

Changing the world view

As learning is a biological need for humans, it is not surprising that it features so largely in our society. Just as animals that are better adapted to the environment thrive, so humans who can learn or invent adaptations to their environment have taken over the earth in a very literal sense. Learning is an important part of our biological dominance, and an essential part of economic development. However, most societies have modelled their education system on the assumption that only some children should be given economic and social advantage. These divisions still exist: in the 5,000 years since writing was invented, we have not yet reached the point where literacy is universal, and new divisions have been created – between those who have access to higher education and those who do not, often depending on their family, race, wealth, social group or religion. It is economically better for all children to be able to learn well, because everyone will gain if the process of learning improves. This is not dissimilar to an economic globalization argument: it is better for all countries to have economic growth, not just the few. This mindset is radically different from the view that countries must outdo each other, that the ill educated are needed to do menial jobs (a version of the argument for slaves), and that only certain people are born to lead. These views are simply uneconomic – and not just politically and morally unacceptable.

The crucial shift of perspective on learning is a shift from conventional wisdom to experimental science, to a new world view about learning and how to support learning – a process sometimes described as a paradigm shift. The change is being driven as much by neuroscience as anything else. The scientific understanding of learning is now possible, and many are becoming aware that things will not remain as they are. Susan Greenfield remarks, 'At the beginning of the 21st century, technology, alongside our understanding of how the brain works and how learning takes place, offers us unprecedented opportunities in learning and education.' The impatience for significant change, driven by this scientific world view, has invaded political and public language. The major challenge is to achieve a fundamental change in our world view of learning, creating the methods of improvement and redefining the outcomes that are needed. The major advances in neuroscience, science and technology are making this shift inevitable.

A cosy and reassuring analogy for the new approach to learning is medicine: using rigorous research methods and fundamental biochemical research to improve health has to be very similar to using the same approaches to improve learning. The analogy is a good one, and to some extent is one people find easier to accept. However, politicians are by no means the only people with strong prejudices about what children should learn and how they learn it: these prejudices permeate societies. In medical terms, good health is accepted as a global right (even if it is not achieved yet), independent of country, religion, ideology, place or age. Good learning too should be a global right that is independent of country, religion, place or age. Some will, no doubt, find ceding what they might see as their right to impose an ideology difficult to accept. Medicine has been abused by the misguided, and the power to use scientific ways of learning to make minds will also tempt the misguided.

Another way of looking at these problems is to consider whether a child, like an adult, should be entitled to freedom from having their view of the world determined by the place they live, their age, or the political or religious system that they find themselves living in. Education now – if not brain washing – is in part an imposition on children of a particular cultural or historical conventional wisdom. Freedom from such societal bias can improve a person's life chances. Children can – and should – be taught skills that let them study different world views and develop their own, and so develop the confidence to live and work throughout a globalized economy. The increasingly mixed backgrounds of communities throughout the world, the pace of globalization and the pernicious effects of intolerance between different cultural groups at the present time all point to the advantages of learning being free from inculcating a particular culturally restricted world view. In general, the right of people to have their own religious, political and social view is acknowledged if they are adult, but not if they are a child. There is no compelling reason why this should be so, and these rights can be ensured in part through legislative means. This argument is thrown into sharp relief when the aim of education is the replication in children of very specific beliefs that create 'an intellectual and cultural dungeon'. This is not just true of the teaching of young children in Pakistan or in Tibetan monasteries but also, for example, in parts of the United States, because groups 'subscribe to a whole variety of weird and non-sensical beliefs [which] . . . they shamelessly impose upon their children'. In the UK the intensely political nature of religious control of schools has been – rather ironically – brought to the fore by former Secretary of State for Education Ruth Kelly, who:

> said the government had to 'stamp out' Muslim schools which were trying to change British society to fit Islamic values. 'They should be shut down,' she said. 'Different institutions are open to abuse and where we find abuse we have got to stamp it out and prevent that happening.' But she said Muslims were entitled to the same rights as Anglicans, Catholics, Hindus and Jewish groups which all had faith schools.
>
> (BBC News Online: 27 August 2006)

For an Education Minister who actively supported so-called faith schools to rail at the consequences of religious abuse of education in those schools is further support for reformers such as Humphrey, who argues cogently that children given restrictive education are, like adults being indoctrinated, having their rights violated:

> Children have a human right not to have their minds crippled . . . Parents have no god-given licence to enculturate their children in whatever ways they personally choose: no right to limit the horizons of their children's knowledge, to bring them up in an atmosphere of dogma and superstition.
> (Humphrey: 291)

This specific argument actually applies equally well to countries, states, religions, ideologies, regions, universities and schools. The global view is that independent learners, with high skills and flexibility, and the ability to analyse and understand various cultures, are better suited to the rapidly evolving world in which our children will live. Human skills or attributes such as self-awareness, being able to manage emotions, empathy with others, motivation and communication skills all seem essential now. Such a different perspective on children lies in the distinction between children who learn to be just like us and children who will forge their own world views from the knowledge and understanding we shared with them. In a rapidly evolving world the prudent parent's response is the second of these: to see their children as independent, and to protect them from cultural indoctrination.

This approach fits in well with the medical analogy of learning, as it creates an aim of good learning that, like good health, is universal, not specific to a society or culture. Equally, the purpose of much segregation in education was to separate children into groups based on difference, but the goal of independent learners with high levels of skills (and, of course, knowledge) is one all can share. The economics of such learning is simple in broad terms: the better adapted everyone is to the economic world, the more productive people are. On a global level everyone benefits if all people can make a better and more sustained contribution. Like good health, good learning is positive. There are elements of how people learn that will never be absolutely resolved because humans will continue to evolve on a genetic level, and the world is one where, to adapt to it, humans need to have a symbiotic relationship with advances in technology and science. In other words, humans will have an ever-changing relationship with human knowledge and the environments they create.

The change described above is one from a largely static education to a dynamic one. If our understanding of the world was changing very slowly, then perhaps merely acquiring the knowledge our parents had is not such a bad strategy. In a rapidly changing world, a dynamic, changing environment requires similar flexibility in education. Yet believing that we need a dynamic process for education still does not identify how children learn, and how we can find out how they learn. Admittedly, solving this problem is no more achievable than gaining a complete understanding of the universe in physics. Yet both of these fundamental problems are amenable to creating a model that can continually be improved through experiment and research to most closely fit the facts as we know them. Adopting the process that has driven the technological, scientific and medical progress of the last century – the combination of rigorous research and experimental science – can achieve the kind of progress in learning we have seen in those areas. The keys to improving learning lie in the combination of the tools of accurate measurement and analysing data – largely looking to refute or refine models of learning – and those of experimental science, looking at the biochemical processes and patterns that are the physical process of learning.

New world view, new methods

Changing the aims and purposes of learning requires new methods to determine how learning can be effective and what the appropriate aims of learning are. The emerging goal is creating independent, highly skilled, flexible, motivated learners regardless of age or culture. The methods will involve more types of learning, more independent learning and links across areas of knowledge, and they will focus on issues impacting on learning such as health. Distribution of learning content can become global, and delivered in different media and on platforms that support learners and collect data. Validating such methods will be rigorous experiments and analysis, and dynamic change will be the norm. These descriptions actually fit some current areas of rapid development, such as ICT.

Accurate measurement and analysing data is essential to the whole process, and a central component in creating a better learning environment. What to measure in learning might be likened to medical measurement, though there are obvious differences. In a simple way, it is easy to tell if people die or get well. But such extremes are rare, and measures of health often rely on proxy measurements (blood pressure and so on) to indicate the quality of someone's health and the value of particular medical interventions. This social science method can work in learning, too. There are also some obvious starting points: use the data already there (health, wealth, attitudinal – as well as educational); use samples – do not test everyone; use experiments; and use the outcomes to locate what works. Social science will be able to create new measures, too, less liable to the failures of current examinations systems where there are well-known problems. For example, examination and assessment organizations do not always use basic techniques of testing such as item analysis (a method of ensuring questions work properly) and there are problems associated with essay-style examinations. *The Sunday Times* reported, 'Bright pupils are being marked down in their A-level exams for giving "too sophisticated" answers . . . rigid mark systems . . . do not take into account exceptional intellectual ability.' This complaint met with the self-evidently false reply from the examination board that 'Candidates will always receive a fair mark for their work'. In the longer term, a process of continuous experiment will be shaped by applying neuroscientific discoveries in learning. The importance of the experimental, social science process cannot be overstated. It is not about effective exams or qualifications but about using the experimental method to improve the understanding and skills of every human being on earth, and giving them the power to be independent learners who enjoy what they learn. These are aspirations, but broadly achievable ones.

The combination of rigorous social science research, experimentation and independent evaluation is not enough on its own. This is because learning solutions that work better than those we use at the moment may not in the end prove the best approach. This is an aspect of the 'QWERTY' principle: we all type on word processors with a keyboard layout that has the keys QWERTY on the left-hand side, despite the fact that it is not the ideal layout. The original reason the layout worked was that it slowed typists down so that old-fashioned typewriters did not jam. However, having become the standard model for the keyboard, QWERTY has become a standard of all keyboards, and better solutions have not been commercially successful. Understanding learning better through social science may involve many QWERTY solutions: answers that only take us closer to the best approach. This approach to improving learning has to be dynamic, changing as the environment changes, using long-term tracking as well as short experiments, and always alive to the tremendous capacity people have to learn, despite the difficulties they encounter.

The creation of a new paradigm for learning is also being driven by neuroscience, discovering the biochemical processes and patterns that are the physical process of learning. The limitations of the social science approach to learning are, in part, that it measures what is, not what should be. It often cannot determine why something works. The long-term goal is discovering the neuroscientific processes of learning: the physical understanding of how to build minds. Neuroscience is already a well-established science, built on biochemical research and its methods, and an established part of the global international scientific networks of communication. Progress is already becoming very rapid, and neuroscientific understanding will enable the matching of learning to the physical dispositions and capacities of the brain.

The experimental scientific approach was created to help move from prejudice and myth towards understanding and demonstrable knowledge. It can be applied successfully to learning, though it may prove a difficult process to implement in the short term. Experimental neuroscientific research offers an aspirational rather than operational methodology to transform learning in the short term – it is not a quick fix. In the short term we need to accept failure and experiment as integral to making progress. Yet whatever we do within this new approach, we will not be controlled by conventional wisdom – rather we will be working towards solutions that will, in the end, enhance everyone's learning.

Giving politicians a graceful exit

Against this vision of the power of science, there are vested interests in keeping education as it is, and even emotional resistance. Perhaps our hesitation in examining what happens in minds as a scientific process rather than a mystery is that it is the last bastion of the belief in our uniqueness as a mystical creature with an exceptional role in the universe rather than as another animal – albeit a very sophisticated one. The history of these ideas might be considered in terms of the growing understanding of the world. Very simplistically, people have: used theoretical logic to create an understanding of things in a content-free area (maths); then applied this to things in the real world (science); then applied these understandings to functioning things (technology); then applied them all to our bodies (medicine – in progress); and now applied them to minds. Suddenly, the era in which people can begin to understand how they learn, how they think and why is dawning and so another – more intimate – area of existence has an explanation, reducing humanity to an understood, biochemical part of the scheme of things.

Some argue that learning is too human for science to offer a better model than the one we have established already. There is no doubt that learning is an extremely sophisticated process, involving the interaction of the brain itself with a changing environment where the understanding of these elements is evolving rapidly. Yet the scientific model of learning is now a realistic goal. The need to understand how people learn and what would help people learn better is driving calls for using a scientific process:

> We need a better understanding of which specific factors are related to success or failure in learning – and in what ways. How do students become competent readers as they move toward more complex texts in subjects such as history, mathematics, and science? What are the short- and long-term effects of specific interventions to help students move from their first oral language to English? Or from oral language to reading and academic disciplines? Why do some students appear to experience so much difficulty moving from concrete mathematical operations (e.g., arithmetic) to the abstract (e.g., statistical concepts like chance and probability)?
>
> (Muijs: 222)

Making these changes through science will need popularizers as well – people who are able to communicate the outcomes of scientific understanding of learning – because the issues are both involved and controversial. There is a need to move the system on – including the political, policy, institutional and education industry as a whole: just because people have access to scientific answers is not sufficient to cause change to happen. There is no turning back: humanity has reached another turning point, for biological science will, in due course, offer a way in which we can understand learning scientifically.

Politically there has to be a way forward from the current situation, and this will differ from country to country. Some politicians might think it safer to avoid the subject, citing the experiences of Dan Quayle, a candidate for vice-president of the US who famously corrected a child's correct spelling to 'potatoe', or Stephen Byers, a Minister of State in the UK, who said that 7 multiplied by 8 was 54. Perhaps politically attractive ways forward are available as a programme of pragmatic improvements. There are four main changes required: experiments in learning, social science analysis, neuro-scientific research and sharing outcomes. A programme of experiments in learning, mainly involving additional learning experiences for children in large structured experimental samples, would probably be seen as a natural approach to the public if carefully handled. These experiments might be in areas of concern – for example mathematics – where a programme of additional learning would be welcome. The experiments would need to aim to find solutions that could apply to all children, rather than just some groups, as this would make good political and social science sense. The quality of the whole programme would be vital, and the infrastructure of experimentation might be based on international networks of research institutions in higher education and medical research, complemented with a new range of research schools. At least some of the learning experiences should not be dependent upon schools at all. The emphasis should be on robust methodology being a matter of course in all areas of learning, as well as those in the experimental trials.

The analysis of the experiments needs to follow a rigorous medical model, but this does not require any government control, only agreed standards, which could be adapted from medical research. This would begin the process of disengaging research in learning and assessing the quality of education provision from the governments' education departments – as it should be. Neuroscience is fundamental to progress, and it is already a well-established scientific field. Additional funding would be appropriate, using international networks already working in the field. The independent evaluation process described above could include those from neuroscience, and ideally a partnership through large international groups such as the OECD could create a global context for assessing outcomes. The direct links between the functioning of the brain and general health would possibly form another research area. The mechanisms for these initiatives are largely in place. Sharing outcomes could use traditional research mechanisms, but – more effectively – go directly to those involved in delivery of learning. There is no reason why the social science methodologies could not be applied in large numbers of schools and other organizations – there need be no dependence on top-down research as the only method.

There are, of course, a range of issues for political consideration here. The logic of downsizing national (or local) departments of education, limiting their responsibilities and redirecting some of their income to research structures will present issues. It will not please some media pundits, policy entrepreneurs and other education experts since their pet theories will, without good evidence, be useless (as one might guess they often are). The outcomes of the new experiment-based system, the learning solutions, need to be shared globally both as information and, potentially, services for learners. It is vital that a critical mass of children and organizations are involved, and that visible outcomes are achieved reasonably quickly (hence the importance of concentrating on issues affecting all children or learners). All of this is manageable politically, allowing governments to present themselves as freeing learning, and putting the customer – the child and family – at the heart of the enterprise. Politics, as the art of the possible, should be able to accomplish the transformation and reap the rewards of improving the service government gives citizens: whether or not it is possible to create the simple, verbless political slogan or sound bite to encapsulate the process is another issue. Perhaps 'a healthy mind in a healthy body' would do as a starting point. The delivery of such a transformation would, however, lie with those actually creating solutions, supported by technology and science.

Chapter 8

The future of learning
with technology

Learning through technology

A scientific approach to learning has similarities with medical research. The medical model is not perfect – it clearly has weaknesses such as the unsatisfactory relationship between the drug industries and medical practice – and similar problems may arise in the tensions between public and private providers of learning experiences. Nevertheless, scientific processes applied to medicine have revolutionized people's lives and will revolutionize people's learning. Technology will play a fundamental role in this process. This is already true of neuroscience and related sciences, as sophisticated technological solutions are needed to scan brains (e.g. MRI), experiment on cells, examine biochemical effects on nervous systems and explore the physical basis of learning in the brain. The tools of this kind of experimental science are those of medical research in the main, and the core discoveries in neurobiology would be impossible without them.

Neuroscientific discoveries about learning have to be turned into learning experiences, and new ways of learning have to be assessed using rigorous social science evaluation. These methods will identify what works in real situations and is affordable. Solutions may be counter-intuitive – quite at odds with our instinctive judgements – but people will have to overcome such prejudice. For example, the idea that economic or social science analysis is somehow foreign to, or even in opposition to learning – the old academic versus working world mindset – is one that cannot survive long. 'Incentives matter' is a key tenet of economic analysis, and it drives all living things, including people. There is a perfectly sound biological reason for this: adaptation to the environment is a mechanism that benefits organisms. This, in turn, will influence engagement with learning: for example, experiences associated with affective incentives are more engaging.

The research process can be carried out by research institutions, such as universities, but also by commercial organizations. As an example, universities probably should move their education departments rapidly into medical sciences and social sciences. Creating a strong university department in this area will take time, but the immediate application to learning within the university itself might prove an incentive. Some universities are beginning to create departments that consider learning in the university itself, going beyond early specialist approaches such as that of the Open University's Institute of Educational Technology, which has examined aspects of learning at a distance for over 30 years. The more difficult tasks lie ahead, as the neuroscience, medicine, psychology, biochemical sciences and social sciences all have a contribution to make to the study of learning, and yet are often still in separate departments. Bringing them together in some efficient organization will be a major task in itself. On the other hand, commercial organizations may focus on short-term answers or solutions specific to their business. Neither approach will make a big impact in the short term, and the capital costs of the technologies required for neuroscientific research alone are considerable. This kind of research will not be cheap, or easy.

Technology and learning

It would be a mistake to assume that technology has little to do with learning: quite the reverse. A case in point is writing and reading, which depend entirely on simple technologies. About 4,000 years ago, Old Babylonians used simple, round clay tablets and a stylus to write. The skill was taught in schools where a master wrote short proverbs on one side of the tablet and the student copied it on the other side. This worked, and the tablets found their way into homes: 'School tablets have been found in almost all the private houses in southern Mesopotamia of this date . . . [this] suggests that in wealthy families all the male children went to school.'

It is shocking to consider that useful skills such as reading and writing were successfully acquired by a whole cohort of wealthy males 4,000 years ago – and still have not reached many of the very poor today. That said, there were pernicious side effects of this initially successful approach, because the method seemed to stifle creativity: 'Babylonian schools [used the same texts for learning and] . . . these texts became part of the curriculum and were still being copied a thousand years later.' The links between technology and new ways of learning have always been strong: adaptive technological tools and processes have not just had physical effects on the environment; they have shaped learning environments, too.

Procedural learning is an important aspect of this symbiotic relationship between technology and humanity. Many technological inventions require procedural learning: musical instruments, pottery, writing, reading, metallurgy, bikes, cars, keyboards and pencils. There are forms of technology designed to support learning directly: the tachistoscope shows an image or words for fractions of a second, and can be used to teach speed reading or test how memorable a new product is. Most significant are the media: print, sound and audio-visual forms. Technologies to recreate sound and visual images have had the most powerful effect on changing culture in the recent past, but have yet to have much impact on learning.

ICT offers new possibilities: digitized media, immense computational power, a wide range of functionality and very fast processing speeds create new ways of organizing and manipulating knowledge. Learning environments can now be interactive, multimedia, ubiquitous and responsive to user preferences or needs. Tracking the user can move from spyware recording use of the internet to learning and offering feedback. This kind of intelligent learning environment is another new contribution by technology to learning, and at the moment the potential of such learning technologies far exceeds the knowledge of how to apply them.

Panacea or practicalities?

New technologies can seem to offer hope for miracle improvements in learning. The history of education is littered with failures based on a new technology: often these panaceas inspire change, and there are short-term motivational impacts on learning. ICT has been seen as a new panacea, but ICT is a tool, not an answer: it is the information embedded in the machines and the communication they enable that are key, not the machines in themselves.

Television is a good example of the potential benefits and limitations of new technologies. There is no doubt about the power of television to influence people – for example, through advertising. By comparison, the impact on learning in education systems has been small. In the US, Children's Television Workshop had early successes, but the initiative was not followed through to other areas of learning. In the UK, the BBC and ITV both created schools television that produced excellent programmes at times, but did not really rigorously evaluate the development and assessment of their output. Even less comprehensible was the failure of the BBC and ITV to work together: each year they created their own schedules, quite independent of each other. In other countries, from Israel to India, the potential to educate through television was recognized, but the actual experiences of learners were based on traditional models – even to the point of broadcasting lectures. Nor did education systems consider that teaching people how to learn from television was worthwhile, even though it appeared it was relatively easy to improve children's learning from television.

There was another set of people interested in learning from television who showed how it could be done well – the advertisers. The most successful adverts focused on a very short space of time (often less than a minute), with high investment in production and entertaining approaches to their audience. The outcomes were often rigorously pre-tested, and also evaluated during the advertising campaign. The best adverts were remarkably successful. There is an interesting contrast here with television news. The BBC began news broadcasts in an attempt to educate the nation, based on radio news bulletins. People may wonder why television news is basically the same as radio news – a person reading a news story, sometimes with pictures. The original reason was merely cost: it was a cheap way of using the same bulletin on radio and television. Later, experiments were carried out without a news reader, and they discovered that the audience would not watch if there was no presenter. On the other hand, when there was a presenter, most of the audience forgot about half of the items by the time the bulletin finished. Further research indicated that a human face was distracting in this kind of learning context, though engaging. So far, news programmes have failed to solve these problems by creating a new format. Advertising can be more successful in getting its message across: the public sector does not have a monopoly on learning or mastering the use of new media.

The media is not necessarily the message: television created mass audiences, and ICT and the internet create mass audiences linked to incredible amounts of information – yet the impact in changing the methods of formal learning has been relatively small. The traditional explanation was that the internet was like having the Library of Congress – with all the books on the floor and the lights turned off. The information is there, but there is no good mechanism to find it. This suggests the education system may have missed the point altogether by investing in unstructured internet access.

The processes through which ICT operates are an object lesson in the creation of new ways of using information, and have lessons for learning. The first step for ICT was to create a global code for information and technology: the digital code (which replaced analogue codes that had also been used). This code is used to create text, numbers, images, sound, databases and many other forms of information. Digital code can be transmitted, stored and reconstructed at incredible speed – and with great accuracy (for example, a gigabyte is about 8 billion individual pieces of information). It is also very easy to modify and change in real time: it is truly dynamic. ICT platforms also offer a formidable array of inbuilt digital processes: procedures for complex mathematics, sophisticated databases, budget management, word processing, image manipulation, information sourcing, and communication creation and management. All these qualities suggest that ICT has a great many tools to support learners, and for creating and managing learning experiences.

In the commercial world, the storage and distribution of information is now dominated by ICT. The intelligent tracking of consumers' interests used by banks, supermarkets, government, Google, Amazon and other organizations demonstrates the potential of technology to support learning. Already there are academic libraries and services that are sold to the learner, and not just formal education in a digital format. A key element in dealing with information in this way appears to be optimizing the effectiveness, efficiency and engaging qualities of the information – not unlike the general characteristics

Figure 8.1 Learning remains social, regardless of the technologies

Source: courtesy of North News

of learning. The unique selling point is the interface of the functionalities between information and people: this is the nexus of the learning process, something the commercial sector found first.

The global language

The transfer of digital information between technologies originally presented seemingly insurmountable complications, and it was necessary to create a global language for ICT. The earliest computers operated on very simple program languages such as early Fortran, with a limited range of instructions ('If x = 0 then 1025'). These languages or codes were both difficult to use and not very powerful. This primitive kind of language has become increasingly more sophisticated:

> http://www.epolitix.com/EN/News/200512/023d561b-2aa
> 4–4438-a1ea-18386a34f415.htm—<HTML><HEAD><TITLE>
> ePolitix.com - Debate highlights education challenge</TITLE>

Most people recognize this as Hypertext Markup Language or HTML. It is really remarkably sophisticated, but conceptually simple. In the example above, the first part is about how to find a single web resource, the second, about what (and how) to display on the screen. The digital code creates a common format for information and processing. The internet uses the global language (HTML and its variants) to communicate information to all technologies. Yet neither the global code nor the global language is what users see. This is an example of the language of computers evolving to change the computer/human interface to seem more human. Our relationship to computers has been transformed by those who realized early on that people wanted to interact with computers on their terms with words in their languages and – later – images, sound and video, rather than through machine codes. An early example of this was when Apple used graphical user interfaces – little pictures – rather than relying on codes and instructions. Everyone rapidly followed suit when companies realized this was a key selling point. The development of computer language is largely a story of evolving to adapt to humans: you ask Google questions in your language, not HTML; you see a digital image, not the code that creates it, and you type into the computer your words in your language. Program developers are working towards a goal of making the use of computers increasingly intuitive, and young users seem to demonstrate that they are achieving that goal. The language of computers has developed out of recognition in our lifetime, and so has their value: I have seen people cry over the loss of their computers – not for the thing itself, but for all that they have stored on it.

ICT is now good at enormously complex calculations, and this has real implications for learning. The random controlled trials of rigorous research are perfectly possible in a sophisticated ICT environment that records the use and outcomes on groups of individual users. This management of data – and the analysis of outcomes – is exactly what individual learners can benefit from: they can find out if they are making progress, and if they are not, how they might do so. It would also be useful to those managing the learning. Examples are the tracking of internet users by spyware, specifically to collect data and analyse how we are using the internet in order to use that information for commercial or even criminal purposes. These techniques of the advertising and commercial world are those that can, with suitable modification, be used positively for learners and others. The power to carry out constant random controlled trials on a daily basis is already with us.

Indeed, the fact that ICT is not making an impact is our fault, not any limitation in the technologies. Rather than seek ICT specifically created for education, educationalists just need to adopt existing technologies, and use those powers in an intelligent way, not try to make them mimic the approaches of traditional teaching in a closed environment. Changing technology does, no doubt, change the skills society needs, and advances in scientific knowledge change what people might learn. That does not mean that technologically delivered learning solutions are necessarily better than other methods, particularly in certain areas of learning:

> Policy-makers should refrain from any further investment in ICT and literacy until at least one large and rigorously designed randomised trial has shown it to be effective in increasing literacy outcomes. Teachers should be aware that there is no evidence that non-ICT methods of instruction and non-ICT resources are inferior to the use of ICT to promote literacy learning.
>
> (EPPI, Torgerson et al.: 8)

The irony here is that this research relied on computer analysis of data, was written on a computer and was distributed through the internet. The reaction against technology in learning can blind us to the considerable changes it has already had on the ways we learn and conduct our lives.

The internet is a formidable technological success, but like printing, the sudden influx of information – and growth of new forms of information – has led to a reaction in some quarters. The internet has certainly meant there has been a quantum leap in the process of sharing information. It has dwarfed the impact of print within less than 20 years. At the same time restricted or hidden activities have become very public, such as pornography, criminality (of many kinds) and gambling: the barriers to misuse are few.

The internet might appear to offer learners world coverage – the link between learning at school, in homes, socially or in wider society – a learning world in every sense. The failure of education systems to use the internet and related technologies is a worldwide phenomenon. In the US, the K-12 movement, where teachers and others created resources for learning in a relatively chaotic way, produced some excellent work, successfully buried in mountains of poor or indifferent attempts to support learning. Some blamed this on the fragmented US education system, but the main limitation was the uncoordinated development of resources based largely on a print legacy. In the UK, the National Grid for Learning and its successor Curriculum Online were notable failures in educational content despite the national curriculum, and the related training programme funded by the New Opportunities Fund (which became a byword for poor-quality training). The use of electronic whiteboards (basically a very expensive electronic blackboard) became a huge UK initiative when it was taken up by Secretary of State Charles Clarke and proved a notable waste of money in terms of its impact on learning. The fault of all of these initiatives, replicated in countries such as Canada, Singapore, Australia and elsewhere, is that they digitized the traditional ways of teaching and the traditional resources. The results were a momentary improvement, perhaps because of the novelty factor for children, but it did not lead to progress.

The current limitations of internet learning are actually those of the publishing world: who creates a quality product that offers a coherent analysis of the world we live in? The answer has to lie in a group of people, organized in some way both intellectually and technologically. In the past this has usually been through books and articles. Some of the learning successes of the internet illustrate just how this can work in practice. A classic example is Wikipedia, an online encyclopaedia created on a largely voluntary basis by contributors. The underlying mechanisms of Wikipedia are technological: you can author an article by following hyperlinks – and the instructions. There are intellectual mechanisms built in, looking at the quality of what is submitted. This does not mean that the articles are all equally good, or equal in quality to those encyclopaedias created by expert, paid authors. However, there is no doubt that the service is a useful tool, and a fascinating demonstration of the power of distributed volunteer networks. A commercial contrast – which is also free – is the very rigorous Wolfram mathematics site, which has definitions and explanations of many key mathematical concepts. For students who use them with the same academic, critical approach they should apply to any source of information, such resources are useful tools, especially when supplemented by those of national organizations such as the Library of Congress, the National Science Foundation and other internationally recognized bodies. There are, of course, commercially available library services that offer electronic versions of print media, such as journals, for both professional and academic groups, and these are already a fundamental feature of higher and professional education.

Learning through the internet faces the challenges of designing learning experiences in any other media: an internet course can – and often does – have all the faults of textbooks. Regardless of the medium through which they learn, people have to be critical users of information (just as they should be while reading or watching television), but at the same time the information has to be appealing and valuable to the learner. Technologies do not solve the problems of education systems unless they are used within a new world view of learning.

This is news to me

The BBC has a world reputation in news and high-quality factual television production. As such, it supports learning through technology in a radically different way than the failed models of K-12, the National Grid for Learning or Europe's SchoolNet. The most important difference is that the BBC is in a market, fighting for its audience with commercial organizations both at home and abroad. The ambitions of the BBC were always global – it has the World Service and is closely associated with the idea of offering an unbiased news and information service to other nations. Originally created to supply content for a new technology (radio), the BBC has relentlessly focused on upward technological compatibility, moving from radio, to television, to digital television and the internet. Its Web services are formidable in scope and ambition, from simple Web pages to streaming sound and video drawn from its radio and television services. It is unique in many ways in having its resources replicated across all the main media (though institutions such as the Australian Broadcasting Company mimic this). Although its services are largely in English, it does offer services in different world languages as well as in the minority UK languages.

The BBC is exceptionally successful, having the highest brand recognition rating of any UK organization. The BBC has been modelled on universal, low-cost access and use on demand in the UK which has, in part, extended to its global operations. There have been failures, such as its foray into the computer business (the BBC B), free internet services by phone and a government imposed limitation on its digital services for schools (which is bizarre). More serious problems have been its occasional conflicts with the government (for example, in 2007 the chief executive had to resign over the BBC's news coverage related to the war in Iraq though, paradoxically, this has bolstered its reputation for independence). The BBC's hypersensitivity about political bias has led to a distinctive attempt at balance in information programmes linked to factual accuracy. The BBC output in factual and information areas has consequently been recognized as striving towards a quality standard not normally seen in media institutions.

The BBC now produces news on the internet, and it is the world's premier news service. The qualities of this service provide a useful model for the kind of learning services that are enabled by digital media and the internet, as well as indicating how they are different to approaches adopted by education systems. Although operating in an essentially commercial environment, the

BBC has been able to maintain strong editorial independence, an ethical perspective and a focus on accuracy – all qualities not always associated with commercial environments. The BBC has, however, learned from the commercial sector, and this is evident in BBC News Online's striking opening page. There is a single-screen home page for news, with headlines and hyperlinks to different areas of interest. The whole is remarkably efficient: the screen is divided into three columns: hyperlinks by place, subjects and language on the left; key headlines (with pictures) in the middle; and additional links on related issues, sites and media on the right. In effect, it offers on a single page a summary of BBC news services, key news stories that day and extended news and wider contextual information. The Web articles are cross-referenced to previous BBC news articles on the subject, giving readers the chance to explore the background to the issue in previous reports. It is a beautifully concise but rich resource.

News Online's use of technologies is also astute: because it is built on short digital summaries and articles, it can be delivered in many formats. Email news, mobile phone news, news alerts, news feeds, interactive TV content, short video clips, radio interviews, podcasts, pictures, hyperlinks – and versions in different languages – are all available on demand. The video and audio elements, drawn from the television and radio services, offer the multimedia experience that communicates in many different ways. In this sense, the delivery of news is built around the convenience of the user, allowing them the choice of what, when and where they wish to access news and information services, and the depth of information they seek. In comparison with other sources of news in print, radio, television and the internet, it is very efficient of users' time, effective in transfer of information, and engaging – as its popularity indicates. It has moved the BBC itself from an institution with a top-down approach to news (decided by the news editors) to a more bottom-up response to user interests. The BBC's use of the internet is an object lesson in quality learning on a global scale.

The use of the BBC News site as a central feature of this book's references and notes is because of the thoroughness and quality of the BBC's services. The amazing achievements of the BBC in capturing the major market share in an international field that includes much richer organizations, in contributing to the wider learning of people and in developing a multi-layered reference resource is a demonstration of the potential power of the combination of digital content and the internet. It is also a possible model to make a substantial contribution to globalizing learning.

The BBC has the potential to offer a distinct, global contribution to new forms of learning as it offers a successful model based on underlying principles. It has high quality standards and high investment in resources. If the support of learning through technology relies on brand recognition, it is well placed. In the process of globalization, the BBC has tracked technological changes, and its services will remain available through different systems. It creates content in different languages, is providing more services that attempt to meet individual preferences, and has a formidable back catalogue. It already has a powerful role in news. As a model for learning, it demonstrates many of the qualities of technologically supported learning: it is focused on the user; it offers delivery on demand, high levels of precision, concision and quality; it is relentlessly innovative; it relies on upward technological compatibility; it seeks a universal audience; and it uses integration with other quality resources.

Degrees of freedom

Thirty years ago the Open University experiment was incredibly bold: to establish an open and distance learning university that would reach all the people that conventional universities had failed to reach. The Open University – or OU – was open in terms of entry (no qualifications were required), methods, place and age – and dedicated to using technology to reach all society. It relied on the expertise of the BBC and the pioneering dedication of staff to create a new kind of university. Over 2 million people have taken its courses (in a country with a population of 60 million), and imitations now exist in many other countries. The Open University takes people without success in formal education and puts them straight into university – and succeeds. It makes the China Central Radio and TV University – the only university in the world that is larger – seem conventional and selective by comparison. Its very success questions the assumptions of education systems worldwide.

The Open University was radical in many ways: it integrated subject areas to create broad-based degrees in a country where 'liberal arts' degrees were essentially unknown. It embraced new technologies and accelerated students through a steep learning curve, building in the skills for academic study into the learning. It created courses through teams of academics, including experts in learning technology, to create a learning experience using a mixture of media (including television, print, sound, face-to-face tutoring and course texts) that could be scaled to any number of students. It was under attack from its inception from those who felt its goals or its methods (or both) were impossible. The Open University subverted most of the assumptions of English higher education by doing away with high entry requirements, residential learning, single-subject degrees, a steady learning speed and courses created by individual experts and delivered in lectures with reading lists, all bundled into an inflexible, conventional pattern of learning.

If so much was changed, and all at once, the Open University should have failed – that is, unless conventional universities were fundamentally wrong about the best way to deliver higher education. Far from failing, the Open University succeeded far beyond anyone's expectations. It was not just the 2 million students who have succeeded in its courses; the quality of education is better than that of almost all English universities. The Open University is one of the top five teaching universities in England, and it has the highest rating of any English university for student satisfaction. *The Times Good University Guide* noted, 'The Open University did especially well on student satisfaction, however, outperforming all the conventional universities.'

From a conventional viewpoint, it seems very strange: students liking better than all others a university that has no separation from the rest of society, no selection, no student bars, no student night life, an emphasis on helping them become skilled independent learners through many types of media and an excellent but online library. The obvious conclusion is that the conventional wisdom about university education is simply wrong. There are other reasons for the Open University's success: the Institute of Educational Technology within the university was a key factor, looking at the quality of its methods and measuring student responses. The Open University's hypersensitivity about criticism from other universities and the wider society ensured quality issues were always important. Like the BBC, the OU had to fight for its very existence, and justify the use of new technologies. Like the BBC, the OU has become a world institution.

The OU continues to innovate. It is the most truly globalized of all the universities: already there is a European network of OU students (managed by its Newcastle region); it has students in most of the countries in the world; there are versions of its courses in other languages; and it is committed to working with other distance learning organizations around the world. The OU operates in a business-like way because it has to attract customers, improving its services and operating a successful business arm. It has recently moved into creating many shorter courses, and delivering courses at different times of the year to suit different students. OU course materials also support other higher education institutions, allowing them to continue to offer subjects no longer viable otherwise. The OU responds to technological change, too, not just in its use of the internet – now an essential element in every course – but in the courses themselves. In less than a year its first all online course, 'You, your computer and the net', became one of the most popular courses ever delivered at university level. In 2007, the OU has begun sharing some of its course content with schools – for free.

New partnerships, new pathways

My own involvement with the OU showed the OU's willingness to venture into uncharted territory. In 1996 I suggested that OU degree modules would be ideal for 16 to 18 year olds in schools, since at that time in UK schools young people did not have access to university study. In fact, schools were specifically forbidden from offering any form of higher education to their students, even if they were able to benefit from a course. As with some other countries, the UK had a rigid dividing line between school and university education: children could go to university early – although this was very rare

– but it was not possible to have a mixture of school and university experience. The OU could deliver its courses to students in schools, so my proposal was possible in principle. The OU agreed on a pilot, which was successful for five years, with students consistently succeeding with demanding independent learning at first-year undergraduate level. After years of negotiations, led initially by Professor Jonathan Brown and later (and in 2007) by Dr Elizabeth Manning, the OU agreed to open the provision up to other schools. We successfully lobbied the government to remove the legal barriers and fund the courses in schools. This was achieved in 2005, ending the segregation of schools and university courses that had existed for almost 700 years in the UK. Now students across the country can mix school and higher education courses, smoothing the transition to full-time degree studies and developing the skills of independent learners.

The change did not stop there. If students began degree studies at 16, the opportunity then existed for them to continue their OU degree while working (as many other OU students do). I suggested to the OU and Microsoft that it might be possible for students deeply interested in ICT to complete a degree in this way. Initially this began as another pilot, with students employed at the school in a proof of concept project. For the students, the degree would be paid for by the employer (the school in this case) – and they would reach 21 with an honours degree, employment in a complex, cutting-edge software environment, and they would have been paid throughout the whole process. For the school, the students operated as high-level technical

Figure 8.2 Under 18 students: a new image for the Open University?

Source: courtesy of the OU, though all students pictured are Monkseaton High School students

support, developing new solutions and running a network of 300 PCs. Everyone gained from the partnership.

It was also interesting to watch two such large, global organizations from different sectors work together. In less than two years the OU had created new degrees that were a blend of their existing courses, new courses and vendor qualifications from Microsoft and others in the ICT industry. The willingness to grasp a challenging innovation and make it work, at one point involving over 400 staff signing non-disclosure agreements, was in fascinating contrast with the stagnation in formal education generally. This new degree opportunity created another precedent: now young people could progress to professional qualifications, degrees and employment skills all at once – and be paid for doing so. The traditional, expensive higher education course – which takes many years to achieve a degree after which the learner still has to find work, learn employment skills and acquire expensive professional qualifications – now faces competition from a faster, cheaper, more flexible – and probably higher quality – option. That it should be created by the world's largest company in partnership with the second largest university is, perhaps, an indication of the way in which large, globalized organizations can create solutions that can be implemented worldwide relatively quickly.

There are more issues that have arisen from this process, as the approach the Open University adopts towards learning is one that can be replicated for younger students: high investment in learning resources created by teams of experts; delivery through a mix of media and direct to the learner; global potential; rigorous quality control built on iterative assessment of learner outcomes; open access for all learners; a commitment to using technological solutions; and a commitment to innovation. In contrast, educational publishing in Mexico is a state enterprise, where the model is a very traditional one of textbooks agreed through a governmental process. Simply having the capacity to create huge numbers of old-style textbooks – or any similar approach – does not, on its own, ensure the organization the capacity to make a global impact.

The Open University is a successful, radical innovation rapidly imitated around the world – in part because it is so cost effective. China, for example, was the country that was most successful in taking up the approach. In 1979, just ten years after the Open University started, China established the China Central Radio and TV University, aimed at those who just missed out on the grades required for conventional universities. The university has programmes for those in work (who have a right to be paid for attending), as well as those who work part time. It is still a selective university and, as the earlier Keypoint schools policy (which created elite schools that selected students by ability) also demonstrates, the People's Republic is still an examination-ridden education system. However, the government is committed to investment in learning and one result is the world's largest university, and a major contributor to the growth in Chinese graduates in the last 20 years.

Interestingly, the China Central Radio and TV University – like the Open University – gives its students choices, and students take more courses in English than at conventional Chinese universities. The fundamental approach of these mass universities is more like a market than a guild approach to learning. Traditional universities limit the number of students on a course, and therefore control the flow of graduates in that area. They police the admissions to their courses, and can restrict social mobility. They tend to use very traditional ways of learning, suited to relatively small audiences. The approach of the China Central Radio and Television University and the Open University is different in kind: here, there is a major investment in learning resources and a reduction in face-to-face learning. The resultant economies of scale drive the universities to extend their markets as widely as possible, rather than restricting the size of courses or their nature. The consequence is a different paradigm for learning: the learning is on demand and delivered to the student; access is largely unrestricted; and the links with the pre-university education system, including its qualifications, are weak or even almost non-existent. Both universities see the delivery of learning through a world language as a key potential selling point for their services, as well as offering scope for versioning their materials into different languages.

Such a radical change in approach in education has been extraordinarily successful, and continues to drive innovation in the higher education sector. It is interesting that the first radical innovation of this kind was in the university sector. This may have been because there was a need to increase the number of graduates rapidly, or simply that the BBC gave the Labour government of Harold Wilson a model: by transforming the informal education of the BBC to the formal education of the Open University it was building on a working model. Whatever the reason, the revolution embodied in these organizations has by no means run its course, nor is it confined to the original models: like the digital arena, mass services for learning may prove to be a highly competitive and dynamic business environment.

McEducate, cooperate or innovate?

The unity of the world's digital environment is, for some, worrying, and the success of institutions that respond appropriately, such as the BBC, is very much the exception rather than the rule. Few people see that in the next 20 years there will be globalization of elements of learning, and many fear a future based on learning (or even education) being in the hands of a few massive organizations. Indeed, the word 'globalization' in relation to learning conjures up an image of 'McEducate' – where what you learn comes from a narrow menu, where the methods are simplistic and where an unvaried diet might make you intellectually limited.

On the other hand, there are the realities of technological development in information handling by companies such as Google. Technology and the internet have fundamentally changed the context for learning, and the tools used are creating global solutions: they are open systems, with greater capacity to store and process information than were conceivable 50 years ago. They offer: lower production costs, increasing value for money and free services; almost instant distribution; freedom to use anywhere, any time; interactivity; and rapid evolution of services and functionality. All of these offer potential, but also uncertainty. Technology has created an open, global, dynamic market but, as the dot-com crash showed, businesses and the public sector have not yet created the right learning processes or content in the right formats to use it properly. The emerging pattern is of organizations operating across different digital media, ensuring they are able to transfer into new digital media (to be upwardly compatible). Many provide digital tools (search engines, software programs) with a direct application to learning tasks, and they offer training – or embed tutorials in their services. They use technology to learn about their customers and try and meet their emerging needs. They work in partnerships, or buy out companies whose services could support their own.

However, the forays of Google, Sun Microsystems and other companies into informal and formal education have not been successful to date. Even universities that are distributing their learning to students are not necessarily making a financial success of internet-based learning. The digital platforms and software are clearly more profitable, and these are directly aimed at offering creative services (word processing, presentations, spreadsheets, databases and other functions). The unique qualities of national education systems outside the US and the fragmentation of the political control of US education itself have, to some extent, limited the impact of the US in formal education for the moment. Yet from Microsoft to Google and e-Bay, the overall pattern is simple: the world's digital infrastructure is heavily dependent on the companies in the US. These companies have global influence, and are the backbone that could enable the globalization of learning. The future of learning seems likely, therefore, to be dependent on US companies, distribution and, possibly, content.

There are exceptions to US domination that indicate that the globalization of learning will not mirror the globalization of the film industry. Non-American organizations such as the BBC and the OU have been able to establish and maintain a global presence in information and learning. These both became national institutions through a Royal Charter – one of the UK's distinctive contributions to the world of public service being organizations funded by the state but separate from it, operating on a business basis and in competition with commercial organizations. The European Union and other government organizations have adopted a different approach: public/private partnerships that, theoretically, bring society together to impact on learning and training. The success of such ventures to date is limited. In contrast, if learning is a globalized endeavour, like medicine, and its processes are shared like scientific research is currently, then it will become a dynamic service for all.

Global platforms can create universal tools for learning and allow learning to develop in a very creative way. Learning languages is an example. The internet allows easy access to text and video in other languages (if only by accessing internet resources in the target language), and there are also a number of very useful language learning websites. There are other advances using voice communication that allow learners to learn directly from native speakers. Skype and other cheaper voice technologies allow telephone projects where learners are linked to native speakers – either peer to peer or instructor to learner. There is evidence that this works well, and produces improvements with only short periods of instruction. Videoconferencing is also a valuable method of bringing a learner into contact with a native speaker.

In such a dynamic marketplace, there are no easy answers. The public/private approach, for example, is hard to manage well. In England, the introduction of a new requirement that all children aged 7 to 11 have to study languages has offered an interesting case study in the use of digital technologies in languages teaching. The government paid a single company about $2 million to create a Spanish learning resource that the company then sold to schools. This has proved only moderately successful and is a very expensive way of creating a resource. This big government approach – linking the government with a major company – proved that financial size does not mean quality or value for money in a globalized business environment. In contrast, the small start-up project for language resources at Monkseaton High School was actually much more successful, and this is not unlike the small-scale start-ups that are a feature of economic growth in many areas of the new economy: innovation can remain alive and well even in global markets. Small start-up companies can take over the world, as Microsoft – just 30 years old – has done.

Intelligent learning environments

A technological environment for learning is not just easy to describe, it is easy to create. Consider this book: I log on to the computer with a fingerprint reader, compose it in a word processor linked to the internet, and interact with friends and researchers through emails. Images, photographs and tables can be inserted into the text, and the entire layout can be changed in a few minutes (I can even have the words counted if I like). I can research companies around the world, order the books I need, and consult government and other organizations. Everything I create is stored, searchable, printable and stored on file servers in a number of locations for security. It is an impressive creative environment that is available to millions of children and learners across the world. There is a receptive learning environment, too, for seeking information – and for learning – such as the BBC News Online. The working environment that created this book is built upon a global, dynamic, digital environment linked to creative tools for writing, complemented by books, people and paper.

This kind of creative/receptive environment can actually sustain student-centred learning through projects such as those used in Liverpool University's medical courses (though there still has to be learning processes and designed tasks created by someone). In contrast, the Open University's courses are an example of very carefully constructed learning pathways, and such modular, sequential, focused learning experiences are still extremely rare. The goal of an intelligent learning environment – one that adapts to the learner's needs and aims – is yet another stage on, but builds on these approaches. Collecting data on people's learning in real time using a variety of methods enables their learning to be tracked. At the moment, data collected by schools, universities and government lacks rigour and is not directly linked to learning outcomes, but this can change.

Powerful ICT learning platforms that track learning effectively and are capable of linking them to learner attitudes already exist. These platforms can take rigorous research and embed it in learning, as well as generating constant, supportive and positive feedback to learners. Such systems can be dynamic, respond to learner needs and in a sense are learning themselves – that is, dynamically improving services to learners. Such an intelligent, responsive learning environment, accessible wherever the learner is, may seem a distant goal, but it is not. Simple intelligent learning environments already exist: the Amazon site that suggests books for you; the Dell PC operation that modifies its demand for parts as its customers order; the supermarkets that manipulate the prices, appearance and shopping environments to maximize profit; and Google's lists of sites that other searchers have used.

Even schools such as Monkseaton High School have created such intelligent learning environments. My vision a decade ago was to create a learning environment that allowed continuous rigorous experiments in a personalized workspace that supported young people's emotional as well as intellectual development. The school was able to partner with Microsoft, which at the time was supporting many schools that were interested in using ICT in creative ways, and the school constructed a new software environment similar to a high-quality business one. This environment was transformed by the design work and vision of Kat Furness, who was a champion of children's contribution to the design of their own learning environments (from digital ones to build-ings) and by constantly listening to the learners – in effect, to the customers of learning services. The user's interface with the system was personal and engaging, while the data system collecting all information about users was, in effect, hidden.

It was at this point that our work was transformed by Professor Daniel Muijs, an international expert in effective schools and assessment of learning. He was looking for schools interested in research, and came to the school, saw the potential of what we were doing, and solved a key problem that we faced: how to measure progress. Instead of more tests for students, he suggested we use a self-assessment system that had been developed in large international

Figure 8.3 Monkseaton students who are close friends created very different learning
spaces

Source: Monkseaton High School home pages

studies comparing educational standards in different countries. It was a simple
but rigorous method that could be applied to any form of learning, and was
backed by rigorous, large-scale research.

This intelligent learning environment works: self-assessments meant
teachers knew children's strengths and weaknesses in the course topics before
the course started, and children were made aware of the topics to be covered.
Afterwards, each could see their own progress, as could the teachers. The
system can measure whether statistically significant progress was made in each
aspect of learning. This allowed courses to be modified, content to be evaluated
and rigorous, controlled experiments to be used. The system can also give
feedback about children's self-concept, their attitudes and feelings. Student
health was also tracked, originally with a European standard for fitness –
EuroFit – as a means to see if students were becoming fitter (or – perhaps more
important – to identify those who were becoming less fit). As this proved
valuable, the system then used a more direct method, a body composition
analyser, initially trialling the system with student athletes. The ability of the
system to add on other sources of information, the inbuilt social science
methodology and the software to then analyse all the information meant the
system could perform in months the kind of experimental research that had
previously taken years – or had been simply impossible.

The real outcome here is that intelligent, adaptive learning environments
are already with us: powerful creative tools; some excellent sources of structured information – as with the BBC; learning pathways, whether student-
based learning or linear (Liverpool or the Open University); and learning
platforms that analyse information on learning, feelings and health. The
combination of all these elements can be delivered to learners wherever they
are, and they can be the basis of creating and improving modules of learning:

a cycle of continual product improvement. The Monkseaton High School system simply demonstrates such systems can be created now from existing software and technologies and do not require a massive national unitary system or enormously expensive purpose-built systems. The underlying methodology enables the scientific method to be directly applied to learning or, to be more precise, a rigorous social science approach to learning.

The real lesson is the need for experiments to improve learning in a rigorous research framework, something that is now relatively easy and cost effective in such learning environments. Professor Carol Fitz-Gibbon, the UK's leading pioneer in this area, recently set out the wider context of this approach:

> Professor Murray Aitken once commented, 'Perhaps the most important thing statisticians should teach social scientists is the need for experiments.' Yes indeed, and if the Campbell Collaboration can have such influence and also reach the political hierarchies, there may be hope that social scientists can, eventually, after hundreds of experiments, become effective in making the world better. If Taguchi can be bothered with hundreds of experiments simply for engineering machines, a few thousand should be possible in engineering a civil society and our children's future.
>
> (Fitz-Gibbon: 4)

Professor Fitz-Gibbon's typical understatement at the end is telling: we are able to transform our children's future with a properly rigorous experimental approach. It is a process, not an answer, but it is a process that has already shown itself to be extraordinarily powerful and – as the Monkseaton High School experience shows – perfectly within the capacity of ordinary organizations. An experimental culture and process on such lines will literally transform children's lives and learning in due course.

Experiment and conjecture

Innovation on its own is not enough to improve learning, even though most innovation initially has a positive effect, as Hawthorne discovered it had in factory production. Changes in how we access information create natural experiments in learning – this is not a phenomenon only found in different education systems. The power of modern advertising is frequently developed through rigorous evaluations of impact on audiences, and the very high investment in television adverts, combined with multiple repetitions, can have powerful effects on product recall and consumer preferences. It is even possible to teach people things that are not in their interests, such as a cult's beliefs or, on a more ordinary level, to buy a product or service. It should be possible to use rigorous research methods to determine how the BBC News Online service has changed the way in which people access and learn from the news. It may be that it is more effective than television news in terms of users remembering more items and content or having a good overview of the news of the day. The underlying point is that learning – in and out of the educational arena – is liable to operate in a broadly similar way in many circumstances, and analysing natural experiments may reveal principles underlying the creation of good learning.

For example, evidence that high investment in creating learning resources can work well is relatively easy to find. The Open University's courses are a case in point, as are the Television Workshop programmes in the US. In both cases, teams of creators were used, formative research and evaluation were undertaken, and feedback from users was actively sought. This process was expensive, but very effective on two levels: that of the level of a single course or programme, and that of the formats developed that then worked in many other courses or programmes. The process was not unlike that of creating a commercial product: work in teams; formative assessment; rigorous outcome measures; a product created so that it can be replicated; mass audiences as targets; and a cohesive set of aims across the intellectual and affective spectrum. The Open University design created a consistent multimedia learning environment, taught the skills that were needed within it and aimed at generating steep learning curves. Children's Television Workshop (the creators of *The Muppets* programmes) tried to blend entertainment, positive social and affective learning, and pre-school learning into a single television series. In both cases very difficult targets were met (improving learning with disadvantaged children through television and reaching those who had previously been unable to access university education). These sophisticated approaches are, of course, likely to be transferable into many other areas of learning.

The use of rigorous social science methods can identify learning needs, assess impact and suggest strategies for improving learning. These methods are now practical right across learning, including working with existing data. Using these methods can be powerful, but though the lessons learned can transfer quickly there can be human resistance for many reasons: fear of mistakes; political, institutional or personal self-interest; inability to cope with the pace of change; and so on. The main barriers are probably the length of time it will take to gain acceptance of these methods as the primary way to judge effectiveness of learning and, on an individual level, the ability to understand or at least accept the methodology. Often rigorous research demonstrates what we may already have suspected could be true – in which case adoption is relatively easy. Major breakthroughs built on a new approach that is counter-intuitive are much harder for people to accept. The use of analogies – such as this book's use of the comparison with medical research to define rigorous research in learning – can help in general terms, but may not when one of the outcomes seems wrong. There will also be cases where the rigorous research is not right, for the methods are those that depend, in the first instance, on probabilities, not certainties. These problems will gradually lessen if and only if rigorous research methods deliver new and enduring success in learning – which they will.

The approach to using technologies in learning that are most likely to work is to build upon the technologies that exist (as advertising works), rather than try to devise technologies exclusively for learning. This is merely pragmatic: it makes such approaches more easily achievable, as well as building upon the learners' existing abilities to learn from or use the technology. The features that are most desirable in technologies for learning already exist: delivery to every home and location; resources in text, sound and vision with repetition on demand; tracking and support; and many tools for learning. This is not true for factors that impinge on learning – health, poverty and social factors for example, or factors in the physical environment such as natural light, ventilation, temperature and ergonomics. There are levels of technological support for learning that can be imagined but not realized yet, such as assessment in real time by biological measures (this is what the lie detector attempts to do – perhaps future technicians will be more successful). What is certain is that technology will continue to develop, and that some of these technologies will offer significant benefits if used appropriately in learning.

There are a number of recognizable themes in learning that are emerging from the impact of technology. The first is very real globalization in technologies, knowledge and, in due course, learning. The second is the fundamental role of experiment within a rigorous research evaluation process. The third is the potential public versus private sector tensions where, like drug manufacture, it is possible for companies to seize on learning as a new product with all the commercial and societal consequences that might have. The fourth is learning content becoming focused on skills and processes in an environment where facts are a given. The fifth is the ever-growing knowledge in many fields that learning experiences should keep pace with, adapt and transmit to learners. Finally, there is the impact of technology and learning on people: people may become more intelligent – as they have already started to do if the worldwide increases in IQ are real. There is an eerie sense that we have reached a stage where technologically supported information storage, processes and distribution – based on networks within and between modules with certain functionalities – have parallels with the biological processes of the brain – and it is to the brain and how to make minds that we must turn next.

Chapter 9

In the end

Learning as neuroscience

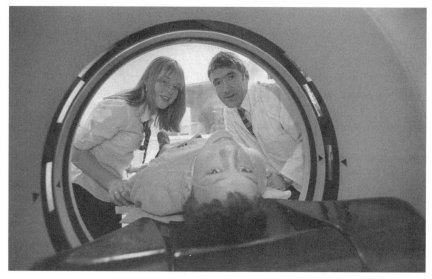

Learning as neuroscience

Learning is a physical, biological process, the ability to modify output adaptively in response to experience. The physical basis of learning implies some basic features of human learning. The first constraint is that there are physical limits to what we can learn as a single individual (though we can learn far more than we do at present). A more sophisticated set of constraints are about how people learn, such as the limits imposed by the senses, though they are not as rigid as they might seem. For example, surgeons can carry out microsurgery with movements that are hard to see with the naked eye, people can understand speech played at hundreds of words per minute, and extraordinarily difficult calculations can be performed in seconds by some savants (or people who train themselves in calculations). The mind is essentially a function of the brain: the brain is the organ; the mind is the pattern of activity within it. Understanding learning will mean understanding the process of making minds.

The structure and function of the brain are the major factors that determine the ways in which people learn most successfully (though the brain is perhaps better described as a set of interacting modules with different functions). Matching learning and learning methods to the brain – discovering what best suits the functionality that exists in the brain – makes sense as a general approach, though it need not be an exclusive one. All of this explains directly why health matters to learning, since the function of any of our organs is affected by our health; why emotion is part of learning, since emotional states and responses are core functions of the brain; and why learning as adaptation to environment has what are called economic aspects and consequences, since economic issues have a direct impact on life styles, health and physical well-being.

The brain's structure emerges from the interplay between the genes creating it and the activity within it. Learning influences these activities, which in turn influence the structure, and consequently allow new patterns of activity to emerge. These changes are physical ones, and neuroscience is the study of these changes and processes. For science in general, the understanding of physical processes is a central goal, and this is also true of neuroscience. Up to now, science has been more successful at determining the genetic codes and how they determine the creation of the brain than at determining the impact of learning on the brain. The full scientific understanding of the brain is, therefore, a long way off, though neuroscience offers the framework for the study of the brain and its functions.

The wider theories of human development in relation to human activity have moved from a social science model such as that of the affluent society (that could free the world of hunger – or let us become fat and selfish) to a scientific and technological model (that could give us understanding of our minds and universe – or let us destroy both). Yet both are based on the premise that human adaptive behaviour can – and does – fundamentally change the environment it has adapted to. The underlying law here may be that the exponential growth in our control of our environment requires an exponential growth in our adaptive behaviours – in learning.

The argument in this book so far is that humanity is entering into a period of fundamental change in our world view about learning and our minds. I have argued that there can be a process for making successful changes based on rigorous experiments. Intelligent learning environments will globalize learning; politicians and conventional education systems will give way to a new scientific approach to learning in which the development of flexible independent learners can be an accepted goal. Achieving these changes is a massive undertaking, but it is not, in itself, sufficient. A process based solely on rigorous social science helps determine what works, but not necessarily why something works – or even what the best solutions are. An analogy might be made with drugs: we create, test and use drugs based on experiments that show they work, but at times we do this without fully understanding why they work or if they are the best solution. This is not the way to understand learning in terms of neuroscience, but does ensure that rigorous evidence is used to determine the relative effectiveness of different approaches. This weakness of finding if a method works well instead of knowing what is the best approach arises from the difference between the social sciences and science in the exploration of the learning process.

Sciences, especially biochemistry and neuroscience, will offer powerful research findings that will, in due course, create a model of learning that explains why things work. The current research suggests neuroscience has reached the point where it has direct implications for learning. Yet it seems difficult to bridge the gap between fundamental neuroscientific research and learning at the moment. There are good reasons for this. The brain is not easily accessible for experiments despite new medical technologies, and the hesitation we have about experiments with learning is nothing compared with the hesitation we have about medical interventions in the brain. The desire to use medical interventions is there, as shown, for example, by giving a largely technologically induced sense of sight back to the blind, or by providing a degree of control over a prosthetic arm. Medical interventions are not new, either: our early ancestors drilled holes in the skull to let things out (trepanning) and not all the patients died immediately. Still, neuroscience often relies on exceptional patients to discover some general principles, and gaps remain between our knowledge of what happens in the external world and our knowledge of what happens in the brain. The neuroscientific understanding in itself changes the model of the brain and learning that allows us to see the mind in a different way: a model of a functioning whole that

> somehow captures the notion of the information processing carried out by the brain . . . cognition . . . refers to the information processing that is carried out by the brain, and lying between the incoming sensory information and the execution of behaviour. [a computer can provide] an analogy . . . The physical hardware of the computer . . . can be compared to the physical brain . . . one can try to design computer programs that mimic some of the essential operations that engage mental processing such as adding numbers, finding a crossword clue or recognizing faces.
>
> (Open University, SD226: Unit 1: 12)

To say that the brain is like a computer is perhaps only to argue that we have modelled the computer on the brain. Other analogies emphasize different aspects of the brain: 'The brain operates like a classical anarchistic commune in which the semi-autonomous work of each distinct region contributes harmoniously to the whole: from each region according to its abilities, to each according to its needs.' This big-picture approach to scientific analysis of the brain offers a starting point for trying to link neuroscience to learning, but the process may be far from straightforward.

Does it all add up?

Considering a specific area of learning might illustrate the complexity of trying to model the process on neuroscientific knowledge. The language of mathematics is truly global, and it is an area that has contributed to many aspects of our understanding of the world around us. Over the past 200 years the standard of mathematics has improved, but still varies greatly between groups. Most people's experience of learning mathematics remains unfortunate. Few people enjoy mathematics, and even fewer feel they are good at it. There have been many attempts to improve mathematics education, and all seem to have had limited impact.

The problems with mathematical education are, on one level, inexplicable. The language of mathematics is exceptionally simple: there are at least 400,000 words in the English language and there are complex syntactical patterns, yet people master this immense system largely through latent learning. There are far fewer than 1,000 mathematical symbols and all the mathematics that we know is derived from relatively few rules – the axioms. Mathematical writing is very clear – yet people appear to make greater progress in language than mathematics. It is easy to see why: there is little latent or procedural learning in mathematics in education; most mathematics at school is presented in a declarative way as rules. The conventional wisdom about mathematics is also a barrier. The issues are not just about how mathematics is taught, but are more fundamental. They are the societal and political fixations on number patterns: adding up and taking away.

The influence of societal prejudice begins with what is taught and when. There are differences in what aspects of mathematics are taught at certain ages between countries and even within countries, partly because there is not the rigorous research on mathematics identifying the underlying nature of mathematical thinking and its development. The beliefs about how mathematics should be taught – the conventional wisdom – extend to the brain, where it is often thought that mathematics has a location – a 'maths centre', so to speak. Yet neuroscientific evidence suggests that, in common with other complex responses that appear to draw on different areas in the brain – such as ethics – mathematics evokes responses from different neuroscientific mechanisms. On the whole, though, neuroscientists are not in a position to tell us much about the mathematical educational process, and for good reasons:

> There are suggestions that children should begin the study of languages, advanced mathematics, logic, and music as early as possible . . . Such arguments claim support from established findings in developmental

neurobiology. However, many neuroscientists and cognitive psychologists believe that current questions about educational practice, for instance, questions about the optimal start of formal teaching, cannot yet be answered by neurobiology.

(Blakemore: 8)

Consider what a very large part declarative memory plays in mathematical education in primary schools: the ability to repeat, parrot fashion, number facts. As my father, Professor John L. Kelley (who taught at the University of California at Berkeley) once said, we spend millions of dollars and years of children's lifetimes teaching them to do sums as well as a $5 calculator – and often we do not let them use a calculator. At the end of the process many of the children forced to try to learn these facts are not able to match the basic functions of the $5 calculator. Despite this, a lot of education systems still insist that children spend thousands of hours learning basic exact calculations, making those children the most expensive and least reliable pocket calculators on earth. One might think that there must be better uses for human lives and human brains than this, that education systems are taking the wrong approach in demanding that children spend so much time on so few facts, and that the way in which number facts are taught is fundamentally wrong.

The role of mathematical thinking in human development is not at all clear in neuroscientific terms. Neuroscientific research is not easy to read at times, but it is beginning to make clear some fundamental aspects of mathematical thinking. For example:

> In the adult brain . . . the left and right intraparietal area, which is involved in visuo-spatial processing, is associated with knowledge of numbers and their relations ('number sense') . . . calculation contains a spatial element. It is believed that this quantity representation system is present . . . in evolution because behavioural studies have revealed number perception, discrimination, and elementary calculation abilities in infants . . . and animals.

(Blakemore: 38–9)

The logic of humans – and animals – having a quantity representation system linked to visual and spatial processing makes perfect sense as a means of assessing nearby quantities of food, danger or distance. Teaching often ignores this quantity representation system in favour of verbal representations:

> Deheane suggests that during development and education the quantity system becomes progressively linked to other representations of numbers, either visually in the form of strings of Arabic digits (e.g. 85), or verbally in the form of strings of words (e.g. eighty-five). Indeed recent evidence

suggests that exact calculation is language-dependent, while approximation relies on nonverbal visuo-spatial brain networks.

(Blakemore: 39)

In one experiment, bilingual children were used as subjects because this
allowed the experimenters to compare the impact of language on exact calculations and on estimation. The outcomes were clear: children were using the
language areas of the brain for exact calculations and the parietal area for
estimation.

The fixation on exact calculation of a certain kind seems to ignore number
sense or estimation. Estimation is a constant part of life: you are crossing the
road and a car approaches – do you cross? You are passing the ball to another
player – how hard will you kick it to be sure it cannot be intercepted? Can you
comfortably pick up the box of books you are moving? In fact, it may be the
most important mathematical skill in real life – but, somehow, it is not so
much part of our school careers. Estimation is an aspect of latent thinking –
often an almost instantaneous response – and exact calculation declarative
memorizing rules and number facts in a linguistic context.

It may well be that children could understand mathematics more easily
visually, building on their estimation skills. For those who have taught young
children (as parents or teachers), it seems obvious that it is quicker to start
with exact calculations using words, probably because they were taught that
way. Of course, most things in real life and mathematics are estimations or
approximations, not neat problems where answers are whole numbers. However, with a class of 30 children, exact calculations help keep children busy
with practice, are easy to test and avoid what can be thought of as the
complicated bits of mathematics. So it might be possible that the problems
that most people have with mathematics arise from an education system that
largely ignores estimation (and the visuo-spatial number sense) in favour of
exact calculation (a language-based skill at this stage in education). It might
be that exact whole-number calculations in early years should be presented
essentially as a way of validating estimations. It might also be that concentrating on language-based skills denies children the immediate success they
might have had using their better-developed number sense skills.

Other evidence raises questions about some assumptions about mathematics. Measures of mathematical ability by gender in some countries seem to
indicate that boys are better at mathematics. The neuroscientific evidence is
not clear about whether there is a difference at all. Large international studies
of children's mathematics make it clear that there are cultural differences or,
perhaps, education system differences. The evidence between countries shows
that boys do better than girls in China, and Chinese girls do better than
American boys. However, when Chinese girls are taught in the US, their
performance drops to the level of American girls. This suggests that they may

be responding to their teachers' expectations, or cultural factors, or the education system – but not to an inbuilt biological limitation. All of this suggests that the conventional wisdom that boys are better than girls at mathematics is probably a cultural or education system bias.

The way to make progress in mathematics is broadly the same as the way that could be employed in other aspects of learning: put current practice under the experimental microscope, and explore better solutions through experiments in new ways of learning. The logic of experimental approaches should derive from rigorous research, and new discoveries in neuroscience – or analogies from known neuroscientific processes. The discussion above suggests areas of mathematical thinking that have been relatively neglected, and they might be areas for improvement in mathematics learning, for example using both estimation and exact calculation as valid approaches to mathematical issues. Another argument is that the linking of different modules in the brain – here, the 'number sense' with the language areas of the brain – could be a conscious area for experiment, such as matching exact calculations as a method to compare with estimation within many activities children experience.

Another line of thought is that the focus could be on establishing an understanding of those elements with the greatest explanatory power within an area of learning such as mathematics. Here, mathematics has identified them – the axioms. The axioms are the small number of central patterns underlying all mathematics: and they are not particularly hard to understand. For example, the commutative axiom is, basically, $3 + 2 = 2 + 3$ and 3 times $2 = 2$ times 3. Not all children know this, even in secondary school. Even fewer understand the axioms of identity and inverses, despite the fact that they are not difficult to grasp. These hardly figure in the learning of most children, which is odd, since they form the basis of all mathematics. Thus, axioms form a logical target for experiments. There are other possible areas, too: mathematical logic – and logic generally – are ignored (partly the fault of some very poor theories that claimed that children cannot not follow logical discourse – when they can). The visual in mathematics is often ignored as well, partly because it has been difficult to re-create the visual world in the classrooms, homes and work – though now this is no longer a problem. These elements could form the basis of focused learning experiments. It would also make sense to review approaches to mathematics that have been tried before but not in experiment-based evaluations, provided they seem to embody features such as the above. For example, in California in 1968, programmes of work for young children tried to approach the first steps in mathematics through set theory, an approach developed by mathematicians keen to establish a sound mathematical understanding for later years. Interestingly, the delivery of the materials also

> tried to introduce each new idea within the conceptual background possessed by the school child at the time he is introduced to the idea.

There is a considerable emphasis on physical phenomena, on experimentation, and other forms of nonverbal and nonpictorial teaching.

(Kelley *et al.*: vii)

All of these are examples of the kind of approaches that could be the subject of experiments, based on neuroscientific research or mathematical logic.

Mathematics could also be taught through non-declarative methods, especially procedural and latent learning and, equally, by establishing not just local nodes of mathematical thinking, but seeking to establish pathways to other areas in science and even language. There are many opportunities to use neuroscientific procedures, such as brain scanning, to map the learning and cognition in mathematics in the brain, and in particular those aspects that involve more than one module within the brain. It may be that focusing on the axioms and central theorems of mathematics may have a similar effect to the training musicians receive in fundamental skills, increasing the myelin around vital neural pathways. In music, this effect is so pronounced that it appears to change the physical appearance of the brain (the professional musician's brain, for example, shows an increased volume of the 'musical' areas).

In general, the process of making minds might involve creating a set of neural pathways that are likely to be fundamental in learning. Ideally these would be the most powerful and frequently used pathways in core learning processes. In mathematics, these might be the axioms and the process of proof.

Learning in mathematics at the moment largely excludes problem-based learning (in the sense in which it is used in Liverpool University's Medical Education programme) and cooperative learning. It may be that technologies can offer new approaches, too: tachistoscopes can be used in the estimation of number, size and other factors. Another example is the experimental approach using induction – that is, finding relationships – rather than deduction from rules you have been told. The physicality of mathematics – whether weights, distances, heights or any of the thousands of other ways in which our three-dimensional world is structured and functions in mathematically describable ways – is often neglected (as is any kind of physical activity in mathematics) or reduced again to digits and signs. Equally, the use of problems that are, in effect, repeated tests gives many children a feeling of failure. There are too many experiences in school mathematics that make children feel they are wrong, and too little emphasis on making progress and being rewarded. Mathematics is bedevilled with a teacher mindset of 'we know, and you do not'. People's feelings about mathematics are often negative, and this is something that needs to be addressed. As with neglected areas in mathematics, neglected approaches to learning are ripe for experiment. At the same time, traditional approaches also have to be assessed in the same framework. On a large scale (that is, sample sizes of thousands), such experiments can offer tremendous progress in a few years, if the experimental infrastructures are in place.

The interplay between mathematical thinking and the body can be further examined with scanning technologies, but experimental approaches can also explore the impact of good health or attitudes on mathematical learning, and suggest solutions if there are problems. What is clear, though, is that the power of mathematical approaches in so many areas of human life means we must improve learning in mathematics. On a global level, mathematics seems the logical starting point for global cooperation, ripe for transformation through research into learning processes, research into the neuroscience of mathematics, and research into the attitudinal and physical influences in mathematical learning.

On the surface, ICT makes it difficult to decide what mathematics to teach – since computers make it easier to carry out the simple arithmetic that occupies most of the time children spend on mathematics at the moment. Like the spell checker and spelling, the basic calculator makes absolute accuracy through mental calculation less important than it has been in the past and other skills more important. Of course, what children learn about mathematics should reflect what they really need as skills – multiplying 238,084 by 294,496 is not a sensible task for children (or, to be frank, anyone else) without the use of a calculator or a computer. The real impact of ICT is in enabling a methodology that can redefine mathematical learning, supporting a scientific process of experiment to determine the best solution, including the technology of neuroscience. ICT can support quick experiments, instant feedback and immediate sharing of outcomes. It can transfer all the teaching materials and resources between schools, homes and countries almost instantly. This kind of support means that experiments to determine what is really the best way forward can be carried out in months, not years. The power of ICT in relation to mathematics – and almost any other subject – lies in its ability to support rigorous scientific experiments, the creation and sharing of content, and global cooperation to find the solutions that have eluded humanity for so long.

Finally, we began to appreciate that the important factor was time

Ultimately a more powerful strategy for improving learning may be to look at building blocks of the brain, including the cells and the biochemical processes within them. On a cellular level, analysis of the single cells is already beginning to create interesting results.

Why study single cells in the brain when there are trillions? The answer is that the function of the brain depends on these cells but is also determined by them – the cells, and their interactions, can only enable certain things, and interact only in certain ways. There are a limited number of kinds of cells in the brain and, though their networks are unbelievably complex, there will be fundamental laws about learning that derive from their functions and limitations.

Therefore, methods of learning that might become part of a scientific model of learning could bear very little relationship to the methods used at the moment. Yet if neuroscientists discover key aspects of how the brain works, or of its adaptation to the environment, it does not necessarily mean that educationalists can automatically apply these discoveries to learning. Such discoveries will need to be put into learning contexts to create testable hypotheses. This might seem an impossible aspiration at the moment, but it isn't: in fact, such testable hypotheses are already emerging.

One fundamental puzzle in learning is how exactly does short-term memory – which lasts less than a minute – become long-term memory. The exploration of our memory established the distinction between short- and long-term memory through our experiences, robust psychological and some neuroscientific experiments. The real problem – on the level of the neural cells – was the nature of the biochemical process that changed a temporary pathway in the brain to a seemingly permanent one.

The educational approach to memory has been essentially trial and error and this has meant that teaching children how to remember things has always been a problem. In experimental science, it is known that people can actually remember thousands of things quite easily. In Leo Standing's experiments people were shown slides with images and words, and two days later were shown pairs of slides, one new and one they had seen two days earlier. They could easily identify the old slides, and could cope with thousands of slide pairings and rarely made mistakes. This recognition memory is different in kind from recall memory – what we might think of as memorizing something, such as a process or formula. The creation of pathways of neural cells was known to be at the heart of the process, but finding the biochemical process that changed the cells themselves was not easy. A leader of the team of scientists that made an important contribution to the final breakthrough, Doug Fields, reported in the *Scientific American* in February 2005 that they had discovered how to make memories stick. The article described how the synaptic connections between neural cells can be strengthened – a process at the heart of creating long-term memories – through a specific sequence. The reported research establishes a model of the biochemical basis of the transfer from short- to long-term memory, and the process contained an unexpected surprise.

For the last 3,000 years educators have been aware that long-term memory often requires some kind of repetition. In education systems this has taken many forms – rote learning, repetition in lessons, repetition over a period of months or years, and other methods including mnemonics (remembering one thing by associating it with a familiar image or word) – all associated with the aim of creating a long-term memory. None of these approaches was a good solution, and not all of them even worked. In biological science, Donald Hebb had theorized as early as 1949 that two cells or systems of cells that are repeatedly active at the same time will tend to become linked (or, crudely, cells that fire together, wire together). The problem of how and why such pathways were created had remained unclear. The reason why was difficult to uncover because it was unexpected, as Doug Fields' team discovered: 'we began to appreciate that the important factor was time.' Specifically, if stimulation is applied repeatedly – three times in the reported experiments – the synapse becomes strengthened permanently, 'but the stimuli cannot be repeated one after the other. Instead each stimulus burst must be spaced by sufficient intervals of inactivity (10 minutes in our experiments).' Blind experimentation and conventional wisdom over 3,000 years had created many methods of memorizing, but it took a rigorous scientific process to find the underlying fundamental law. Fields was quick to point to the consilience with Hebb's theories and its adaptive function for humans as:

> it offers a very appealing cellular analogue of our everyday experience with memory . . . one does not always know beforehand what events should be committed permanently to memory. The moment-to-moment memories necessary for operating in the present [are managed] by transient adjustments . . . but when an event is important enough or repeated enough . . . fire[s] neural impulses repeatedly and strongly, declaring 'this is an event that should be recorded'. The relevant gene turns on.
>
> (Fields: 65)

So, having identified a fundamental process – whereby stimulation to create long-term memory had to be repeated three times with gaps of ten minutes between – this biochemical change appeared to be a testable hypothesis.

It occurred to me that it would be possible to try to create a learning sequence based on Fields' discoveries. I consulted Dr Terry Whatson of the Open University who agreed it would be possible, though we both felt it could be extremely difficult to transfer a fundamental cellular law to actual learning in a traditional setting.

These ten-minute gaps between each stimuli were quite at odds with any method used in education as far as we could discover. At least it had the advantage that it would be easy to compare it to other methods. I decided to explore the possibility at Monkseaton High, and Angela Bradley, a Science teacher, took up the challenge. We decided to stick rigidly to the ten-minute gaps the scientists had used. We designed an hour's lesson on the human heart with three sections we hoped would offer a similar stimulus – a carefully prepared presentation (created by Angela and a group of three students) with a variety of ways for the learners to respond but covering exactly the same information. This could be repeated three times separated by ten-minute gaps. The presentation included names of chambers, the functions of valves, double circulation and processes carried out by the heart. Following Terry Whatson's advice, the gaps were filled by physical activities unrelated to science, so that the same area of the brain would not be stimulated. We had every expectation that it wouldn't work: students wouldn't respond well to such an unusual lesson, and the attempt to stimulate one particular set of nerves was too complex to try in such a simple approach. It would be a proof of concept trial: could it really be done? We delivered the lesson to about 80 14- and 15-year-old students and compared their results with controls. We found that learning could be delivered in this way – students found the lessons 'different, but interesting'.

The next stage was to see if it would work with students who were a different age. I taught the lesson to a group a year younger – two years before they needed to master the material according to the English examination system – and tested them with a formal examination question. Their results showed they could master the complex material just as well as the older children in just 24 minutes (not counting the ten-minute gaps, of course). I found the experience a little unsettling: it made me consider how much time is wasted in education, especially since the children remembered so precisely what had been presented to them.

We then changed the subject to bacterial resistance and evolution and changed the form of the test to multiple choice. Further, we mixed the forms of presentation to produce three approaches: traditional teaching, teaching with gaps, and teaching with gaps plus conventional teaching. This last pattern used the teaching with gaps, but put traditional teaching in the gaps using very different methods of delivery (social, personal responsibility responses, but on the same topic). This would, in theory, lead to interference with the synaptic changes, but only to some extent.

The lessons were given during the same period on the same day, taught by teachers who did not normally teach those classes, thus keeping the variables between lessons as few as possible. Two weeks after the lessons were taught the post test was given. There were no significant differences between groups in terms of potential, achievement or subsequent performance in an actual GCSE multiple-choice Science examination on different topics.

The results again suggest the effectiveness of the experimental approach, as the Table 9.1 shows.

The learning efficiency measure gives an indication that the gap method works at very high levels of significance. Of more interest on some level is the mixed group. A key assumption of gap learning is that there is no stimulation of the target neural pathways in the ten-minute gaps. Traditional teaching of the same topic, however different in approach and focus, would theoretically impact on that learning. If there were no interactions that interfered with learning, then this group should have the learning benefits of the experimental group, and an additional element of traditional teaching benefit (perhaps at the same rate as the control group). In fact, learning was near that of the control group. It appears there had been interference, in line with the neuroscience model. Further experiments here confirmed these outcomes.

Table 9.1 15–16 year olds, experiment 2

Experimental model and control group (n = 55)	Academic potential Yellis*	Learning efficiency (learning per 60 minutes as measured by the test)**	Significance (experimental v other approaches)
Experimental group (24 minutes teaching)	4.9	173	
Control group (60 minutes teaching)	5.0	61.1	F = 23.84; t = 6.90; P < .001
Mixed group: mixed approach (60 minutes teaching; 24 minutes as in experimental group; 36 minutes conventional social-based methods)	4.9	75.2	F = 16.83; t = 7.61; P < .001

Notes: * The UK's best measure of academic potential: higher scores being better. ** A new form of English Science examinations, introduced in 2006 (reducing the possibility of prior learning in the groups)

The results of these trials are not conclusive, of course. However, they seem to suggest that the gap method works – children can learn with timed gaps of doing something completely different (and, no doubt, doing nothing at all that is 'educational' in the traditional sense). This kind of experimental process of transferring neuroscientific discoveries to actual learning experiences suggests fundamental laws from cellular research may have a direct application to learning. The rhythms of learning may be based, in part, on timings in cellular activity that create neural pathways.

Doug Fields and his team have not limited themselves to the neurones, and have also considered myelin – the fatty substance that can grow around neural pathways that are repeatedly stimulated. Experts in sports have often said that it takes ten years for a child beginning a sport to become world class. It now appears that what is needed is constant practice of basic skills, improving fitness, as well as practising the sport itself. It means time practising skills, and that time means repeatedly stimulating key neural pathways, and the growth of myelin around those pathways. What good could this possibly do for the athlete? The answer is quite simple: myelin insulates a neural pathway, allowing it to transmit messages more accurately, and faster, just like insulating an electric cable. To become world class, you must practise skills. Fields comments: 'getting good at piano or chess or baseball takes a lot of time, and that's what myelin is good at,' or, if you like, genius is made by time, and within the brain by reinforcing key neural pathways, whether to create a genius in music (like Mozart), or in games.

This led me to consider the secret of Monkseaton High School's football team – a complete mystery to me as an American. The team had an entire season without defeat, and became English Under 18 champions. In the same year, students from the team were offered football scholarships to US universities worth $1 million in total. The secret, if any, was time, and focusing on key neural pathways (or skills): the coach, Danny Olson, treated them like professional players, with lots of fitness and skills training, and relatively few matches. They trained 21 hours a week, 6 days a week, 41 weeks a year. They were even tested by new medical technologies to reveal areas where they could improve their fitness. Perhaps they were also building myelin insulation.

The technologies used with the football team were based on body analysis through impedance testing: small currents passed through the body that identified muscle, fat and other tissues. If it was useful for footballers, why not with everyone? I tried it myself, and discovered I needed to shed 4 kg of fat and had few muscles to speak of in my trunk. Over the summer I tried to exercise my trunk and take care with my diet, and tested myself again. Success – I was making progress towards being healthier (only 2 kg of fat and some more muscles in my trunk). I felt I knew what to do, and could see that it made a difference. I still weighed the same amount, so my BMI (body mass index) was the same, but I was actually fitter and healthier. I was pleased – and if I felt like that, wouldn't young people?

So we started the same testing with many young people in the school, and a trial group was offered an 18-hour programme of physical training to increase their general fitness and reduce unnecessary fat (bearing in mind that fat is, after all, necessary for good health). The programme included advice on diet, and was very different from traditional PE lessons. The activities were aimed at specific changes (including increasing muscle mass) based on the body analysis testing. The results were striking: their fitness increased dramatically, and for everyone – despite at times an increase in their BMI – the percentage of body fat decreased, and muscle increased. It was simple, effective and practical. Methods that worked on professional athletes could be used effectively on anyone, and the efficiency of the process – the benefit for every hour of involvement – was impressively high (Figure 9.1).

Like Doug Fields, Russell Foster is not a name well known in the educational world. Yet these two neuroscientists may be far more important to improving learning and education than most of the educational experts that have ever lived. Doug Fields has shown the importance of time in the patterns of learning; Russell Foster has shown that the rhythms of life – the biological clocks that control so many aspects of all living things on earth – dictate the importance of times for when people should learn. And both realize the importance of communicating these findings to the wider world.

Russell Foster has drawn attention to the mechanisms in the brain that create a circadian rhythm in our lives (that is, the 24-hour pattern based on

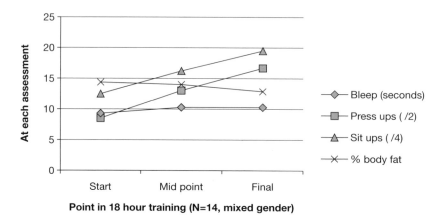

Figure 9.1 Focused fitness training has significant impact (p < .01)

Source: Monkseaton High trial data

night and day). On the surface, there seems nothing unusual about that, but the neuroscience of the process is not at all what might be expected. The first surprise is that the cells of the eye – the rods and cones – are not the only light-sensitive cells in our eyes. There is another kind of cell, and it reports to a very small part of the brain now called the SCN (the suprachiasmatic nuclei). The SCN is something we share with other mammals, and it controls circadian rhythms – our 24-hour clock. The next surprise is that the SCN is not something that we can influence – it is responsive to light, but not to training or our will. Whether we will or no, we are bound by the natural rhythms of day and night.

The circadian rhythms that are established might seem to be changeable by using electric lights and, besides, how does it really matter? Foster gathers research papers from around the world to demonstrate that it matters a great deal. Our hunger, our learning and our health are all influenced by the circadian rhythms: for everything there is a time, and that includes learning. This is, however, by no means the most important conclusion for schools and universities.

A central point about circadian rhythms is that they change with age in humans. We have always assumed that learning early in the morning is best, probably because it is best for young children and adults. Unfortunately, it is not true for teenagers. In fact, Foster might be the person who is most likely to destroy our understanding of teenagers: 'Are we at our most alert in the morning? In the case of young adults the answer is no . . . in fact that may have a detrimental impact on their ability to learn.' Our SCN dictates that at about the age of 12 we begin a journey in time, where morning – for our hormones and our mind – begins later and later in the chronological day until, in the late teenage years, it begins two hours later than for everyone else. Of course, there are variations for each individual, but until 19 for women and 20 for men, our neurological alarm clock drifts later and later. So when teenagers are woken up at our morning time, their brain tells them they should be asleep. So they use stimulants, such as coffee and cigarettes, to get themselves awake. But at night, when we go to sleep, their neurological clock tells them it's not time to sleep, so they drink alcohol or take drugs to get to sleep. The next day, it's the same pattern; so many teenagers become sleep deprived because they cannot control their neurological clocks. And that makes them surly, irritable and, unfortunately, more susceptible to illness and other problems.

These are the kinds of problems also faced by night workers, but for teenagers and their parents there has never been an explanation of teenagers' behaviour, or of the effect of trying to get them out of bed in the morning – when it is the right time for the parents to start the day and the wrong time for the teenagers, according to the neurological clocks in their brains. School and university only make things worse: 'Teenagers show both delayed sleep and high levels of sleep deprivation, and these problems have been largely ignored in terms . . . of the time structure imposed on teenagers at school.' And Foster goes on to point to the medical consequences: 'Long term sleep deprivation might contribute to . . . conditions such as diabetes, obesity and hypertension – which are now alarmingly common in the young.'

The importance of neurological patterns of time as a factor in our learning and our lives has been largely ignored. Our brain controls both the rhythms of learning and rhythms of night and day that, despite our technologies, continue to order our lives. We need to fit learning to these patterns of time.

Finding the keys to children's futures

Using the scientific method in learning applies not just to the methods employed, but to the content. The comparison between textbooks – often largely the creation of a single author – and the materials from the Open University or publications in scientific journals make a basic contrast clear: major investment of human expertise is an essential part of creating knowledge. This principle, combined with the ease with which factual information is now accessible, gives some indication of how the day-to-day experiences of learning might evolve as the understanding of learning grows. These are complicated issues, and it is likely to take many years before it is possible to unravel the system we have inherited. Since learning is the development of adaptive skills – adjusting to our environment – then an appropriate goal of learning seems to be to create independent learners engaged in the learning process and with a wide range of skills. To achieve this kind of goal it may well be best to focus on fundamental laws and procedures. A starting point is to identify the most important things to learn: those with the greatest explanatory power or the most useful procedural skills. These core laws and processes already underpin our social adaptation to our environment and would give a coherence to what is learned.

One shift in emphasis in such an approach is from content as fact to processes. For example, the scientific method is a common approach to many different areas. Even very young children understand that scientific method helps us find out about the world, even though the words they might use to describe the processes are simple. A young child might understand 'now make a guess' and then use a fair test to see if it is true, and that is a process children quite often enjoy. Yet it is a powerful method that can be applied in many areas of children's learning. The same is true of the building blocks of mathematics – the small number of axioms that are the basis of all mathematics. They are easy to grasp. The harder part is to use them in proofs, something that is usually reserved for degree-level study. Again, there is no reason to do so: children are interested in why and exceptions. The historical purposes of education systems distort what is currently learned: the need for clerks and officials who could act as calculators drove the fixation on number facts, and made some sense, 100 years ago – it does not now.

A focus on processes and fundamental laws would change the look and feel of learning. However, the laws and processes would give children structures that work in many areas of knowledge – the kind of mathematical thinking lacking in their education in most countries, the kind of scientific approach that is usually abandoned for facts and the critical approach to knowledge that is essential in adult life. These changes are, of course, only a small part of the changes that may occur. For example, there is good reason to think silent reading is important – the latent learning of formal or creative prose and the reinforcement of the neural pathways supporting reading suggest this, as does earlier, if inadequately rigorous, research. This does not mean small moments of reading from textbooks, but extended periods, and formal education has not made a place for this central skill (partly because it is hard to organize and assess in current education systems). The list of possible changes is long. Examples might include: greater emphasis on children's creative, communicative and social skills; opening up education systems to interactions with the wider world; cooperative learning; better physical environments; focused health support; economic support for families and communities; and even real work (one could imagine a school or university run with learners – even paid learners). One persistent issue has been cited as a fundamental research question for neuroscience:

> The brain's limbic (emotional) system is different from brain systems that process academic abilities, but they are strongly connected. Does learning skills such as reading and writing and maths affect emotional development and vice versa?

(Blakemore: 42)

The answer to this appears to be 'yes', but the need to create a better, more human environment in learning seems a fundamental goal. There are also issues about the extent of formal learning – as well as its nature: it should be efficient as well as effective and engaging: there is no need to use a long time when a short one will do. All of these arguments point to the scale of the task that confronts society in improving learning.

The principle that important learning (and possibly all learning) should be based on a major investment of human resources on a global scale seems inescapable. One possible strategy is to use teams of children and teachers as creators. This was the approach with the heart presentation used to test the ten-minute gap theory described above: Karl Rennie, Vadim Petrov and Thomas Derby (all aged 16 at the time) tried to embed certain qualities in the presentation they created – clarity in the theories, with absolute precision in presentation and language – and to make use of feedback from teachers and other learners to improve the presentation they created. They felt a sense of responsibility to others, and tried to avoid the faults in the materials they had experienced in classrooms. The content they created seemed to be effective, efficient and engaging, and this tends to support the argument of Professor Carol Fitz-Gibbon that peer tutoring – children teaching children – is a very powerful method to assist learning, though by no means the only approach.

Making minds by changing the functioning of the neural systems in the brain should be helping children to adapt to their environment. We have to take the greatest care about what they learn; we must not simply stuff things in that adults learned when they were in school, or merely occupy children's time so that they are not troublesome. This has been intuitively perceived by many:

> a . . . brain originally is like a little attic . . . A fool takes in . . . every sort he comes across . . . knowledge is at best jumbled up with a lot of other things, so that he has a difficulty in laying his hands upon it . . . the skilful . . . is very careful indeed . . . nothing but tools which may help: . . . a large assortment, and all in most perfect order.
>
> (Sherlock Holmes in Doyle: 21)

Perhaps fundamental laws and processes, including creative and emotional ones, are fixed points for learning. Building these would establish robust tools or skills in the learner's mind that can be applied to many different areas of knowledge and experience. The brain works in networks, and the networks that learning establishes must be those that have the greatest benefits for the learners.

This said, how the processes and laws are learned (whether using ten-minute gaps or a similar approach based on the brain's functioning) has to be subject to rigorous research too. The content used in learning also has to be based on sound evaluation and experiment. All of this will take time, but the construction of the minds of children – which, as we know, actually changes the physical brain itself – should no longer be the province of the amateur or politician, nor is embedding our prejudices in children compatible with their rights or our responsibilities.

Learning based on neuroscience will lead us to a point where we can find better methods and make wiser choices about what children learn. They can learn faster, enjoy the process, and be better adapted to their environment. All of this is achievable, but learning is only part of a child's life, and it has to be seen in that wider context. If we are making minds, we are also making lives, and a child's self-concept, health, economic potential and other outcomes are all affected by their learning.

Education can make children drug addicts: what should learning do?

The current education systems – particularly in the US, but also in some areas of Europe and elsewhere – are still part of a growing children's drug market (and, incidentally, plastic surgery market). These are not just the traditional drugs, such as alcohol, cigarettes and heroin, but drugs created to change children's behaviour. Not all of them are as addictive as more traditional drugs, but children and parents can become dependent upon them, and thus they make a good commercial product. The understanding of the brain has led to more and more ways of trying to directly influence behaviour. Nor is it just one drug – such as Ritalin – that suddenly became the drug of choice of educationalists, parents and children. As Professor Steven Rose, a neuroscientist who specializes in memory, points out, there is 'a variety of other drugs . . . being added to the torrent now being enthusiastically and quite legally poured down children's throats'.

The process here seems logical, but is actually commercial: parents worry about their children, and the drug companies respond with a product. In this case, the label that is used is ADHD – attention deficit hyperactivity disorder – a set of symptoms that might be described by the harsh as another way of saying 'naughty but often bright children'. The underlying process seems to be that parents feel their children are misbehaving, or not conforming to the cultural norm. Any description of the problem that puts the blame for this on some chemical reason – rather than bad parenting, bad education or some form of neglect – seems a better option for the parent. The industrial response is straightforward: if there is a set of symptoms that are socially unacceptable, they will find drugs that mask those symptoms and, at the same time, offer a justification for the problem that parents (and, indeed, children) can accept – it is not the fault of the people, but of some kind of chemical imbalance. These approaches are bad science in two ways: first, they measure a problem through estimates of normality and, second, they ignore the rigorous evaluation that points to other likely causes: the 'diagnostic criteria . . . the description of the behavioural problem is of its nature relational, in that it requires comparison of the child being diagnosed with other children of the same age, background and so on'. There are many problems with this, but Professor Rose in his recent impressive review of neuroscience *The 21st Century Brain* concludes the Ritalin-type 'methodology . . . is deeply flawed'. Rose's central point is not that such drugs are based on poor science. He notes that marketing methods ensure 'Huge increases in diagnosis and drugs (mainly Ritalin – as in the US)'. Yet his essential point is simpler: 'Ritalin no more "cures" ADHD than aspirin cures toothache.' The problem is that the socially unacceptable behaviour of children in school is not seen as a problem possibly created by schools and the formal education system but as one that must be repressed. This repression of what some elements in society think of as undesirable is a familiar theme in history: from religious persecutions to invasive surgery on those of different races, people in control have tried to use medicine to control others. Rose spots the fundamental problem of trying to solve problems in schools and education through drugs: 'we will once again find ourselves trying to adjust the mind rather than adjust society.' The history of behaviour thought of as deviant by those in control supports this analysis. Methods that stop such behaviour include lethal injections, electroshock therapy, pre-frontal lobotomies, barbiturates and so on. All this derives from seeing the brain as a simple organ where physical or chemical quick fixes are appropriate. The treatment of depression by Prozac and other drugs is another attempt to block symptoms rather than cure illness. These expensive and profit-making drugs are part of an industry that is not always well regulated: 'in December 2003 it was reported that some 50,000 children and adolescents in the UK were being treated regularly with a variety of antidepressant and anxiolytic drugs, often unlicensed for use with young people.'

A drug is by no means the only – or best – solution: for example, there is clinical evidence that depression can be alleviated though talking to patients in a structured way. Many other cures depend on implementing programmes or rules that change the person's social environment. Some of the more entertaining, if less scientific, are reality television programmes such as *Supernanny* or *Honey We're Killing the Kids* where naughty or unhealthy children are reformed by an outsider modifying the way the family operates day to day, establishing new social rules or changing their diet. Really dangerous behaviour can be mitigated through non-medical interventions too, as the Surgeon General's report on youth violence seems to demonstrate.

It would be reasonable to argue that until society can produce a more rational and dynamically improving learning environment, trying to enforce learning through drugs is simply not appropriate. It also seems that attempts to increase the power of memory or other brain functions through chemical interventions are almost certain to have side effects. As learning becomes an explicit process of making minds that are as functional for the individual within their environment as possible, questions will legitimately arise of the role of chemical interventions. I think the answer to this question raises ethical issues that lie at the heart of learning. The division that has always existed between medical practice and education was easy to maintain when there seemed no connection between the two. Now it is known that learning is a physical process and that medical interventions can have related – though different – effects, there can clearly be overlap. An initial conclusion from recent experience is that educational judgements of maladjustment or disruptive behaviour are not adequate for medical diagnoses, and should not be used as the basis for medical treatment. An ethical argument supports this: the purpose of learning is to enable independent learning and judgement, not conforming when institutions provoke the behaviour they condemn. In the end learning should make people free, and corrective drugs (and possibly surgery) make people dependent, so these medical inventions should, in general, be avoided. I rather suspect that you do not learn anything by taking drugs. The more perceptive neuroscientists have seen the two pathways here as a fundamental research question:

> One day we might be able to take a drug to improve our learning and memory. Alternatively, different types of . . . [learning] might have the same effects as taking a drug in terms of the chemical systems in the brain.
> (Blakemore: 31)

Good science will need to measure all the factors that might influence learning as well as the nature and methods of learning itself. Clearly possible factors include children's attitudes, self-concept and health, as well as their social and environmental circumstances. Medical interventions that improve general health are clearly appropriate as a means to improve learning, and there may be specific interventions to solve medical abnormalities in the brain – but controlling children with drugs is not appropriate.

Finding our way

There are many theoretical models for learning, but convincing evidence to support them and the fundamental patterns in learning as yet remain unclear. As this changes, patterns will emerge that will create a better model of human learning. These patterns might be about knowledge, physical changes in the brain or children's motivation, feelings and attitudes towards learning. As argued earlier, learning has to be a good adaptive response to the current and near-future environment. Equally, learning does not occur in a vacuum: there are major societal issues about learning that include economic pressures, the human and physical environments for families and employees, and society's changing needs. This does not begin to touch on the research necessary to create a real understanding of learning as neuroscientific processes. The challenge is to create as accurate a model of learning as possible; the capacity to manage the ever-growing demands of knowledge transfer within an increasingly complex society; and a humane and enjoyable environment for all people (from children to employees) that would achieve those ends.

Taking one possible pattern might help to show how a number of different aspects of learning might prove to be related. It seems to make sense in almost any human endeavour to be efficient: to use as little time and resources as are really needed for any outcome.

The first logical outcome would be that being concise is best for learning – that learners are presented with what is essential. This relates to learning quickly, but has the advantage of removing elements that could be distracting. It makes the ability to go back through a learning experience (whether in a book or online) more important. This tallies with most people's experience of good teachers, books and online content: they are very clear and make even intricate things seem simple. In neuroscientific terms, precise learning would possibly require the fewest cellular pathways or cellular resources.

The second outcome would be that when learning processes, having as few steps as possible in each process is best for learning (for a counter-example, in a famous experiment with pigeons, Skinner, the founder of modern behaviourism, showed that they could learn a sequence of actions, but occasionally put in extra actions that had no purpose, such as turning around 360°: the pigeons appear to have thought it was necessary; we know that it wasn't).

The third outcome would be that being precise is best for learning: the absolute accuracy of materials is important. This would radically change some learning. Often children are presented with simple models or arguments that are actually not true (and that they then have to unlearn later). There are many examples in science teaching and mathematics. For instance, children are sometimes taught that '3 into 8 does not go', implying you cannot divide 8 by 3 – which of course you can. A more sophisticated example is that children are told that objects are red, rather than that those objects reflect red light. Being precise requires an academically precise explanation from the beginning (which is, of course, not the same thing as a full explanation). Again, this chimes in with good learning experiences we have had – precision and accuracy from the beginning help avoid confusion later in learning. It also makes sense in neuroscientific terms: create pathways that can be reinforced over time, rather than pathways that have to be replaced by alternatives.

The fourth outcome is that learning that is most widely applicable is best for subsequent learning. This is fairly obvious: learning effectiveness is often best achieved through learning patterns and models that can be applied in many different ways. This maximizes the speed of learning as well as linking different areas of knowledge. In neuroscientific terms, learning that improves adaptation to a range of things in the environment, rather than one, is likely to be efficient. It does mean that learning is hierarchical – not all learning is equally valuable – but it does not mean that all learning is sequential (you must learn things in a specified order).

These arguments may link directly with neuroscientific realities. The brain may have a tendency to operate as efficiently as possible, either by using the shortest possible appropriate pathways or by using existing functions to achieve new ends. It may imply that in adaptation to the environment the brain has a tendency to obey a law of least effort. It may be that this is a variation of Ockham's Razor – the general scientific principle that the simplest solution is the most likely to be true.

The law of least effort and the possible outcomes described above are, of course, merely conjectures. Providers of learning, such as schools, can use rigorous research methods to carry out experiments on conjectures such as the above, innovating to improve their service to learners. They can act as centres for research and development and, as in good medical practice, seek, validate and share good learning innovations. This experimental approach has the practical advantage that it is simple, quick and rigorous and can be widely applied now. Examples of innovations give some idea of what can be done quickly. Teachers and pupils might identify weak spots in learning, where pupils are known to have trouble making progress. For example, children have trouble understanding Shakespeare texts or similar historical texts when they first encounter them. What are the most efficient ways of approaching the text initially? Seeing a scene acted? Just hearing and reading it? Acting it out? Having all the words or phrases they do not understand explained first? Interacting directly with the text in a particular way? There may be different answers for different groups of children, but that does not alter the fact that there will be more learning if we know which approaches are most effective. Other problems are the curricula themselves – they are wrong when they require children to learn things that are too hard – or too easy – or have elements that are inappropriate and inhibit progress. In other words, there are barriers to progress that are not the fault of the child, the teacher or the school – but of the imposed curriculum. More intriguing issues can also be explored, such as the relationship between health and learning. Do unhealthy children make less progress and does becoming healthier lead to making more progress? These are all issues that can be addressed with this methodology of rigorous experiments.

Neuroscience will generate new knowledge and hence testable hypotheses about learning. The experiments described earlier for creating long-term memories using ten-minute gaps are of this kind – and these, when much larger samples are used, can identify solutions to improving learning where the neuroscientific discoveries are directly linked to the outcomes. These neuro-scientific experiments may be quite complex, but they are already showing how elements we often thought of as separate (cognitive learning, emotion and health, for example) are really aspects of the brain's function in learning. Steven Rose summarizes the research to date as follows: 'First, emotional memory is more powerful than purely cognitive; and second, that body and hormonal state affect how well something is remembered.'

The conclusion strikes at the heart of current education practice: learning is a function of cognitive, emotional and body/hormonal state, and therefore the learning process needs to explicitly involve all these factors. Some of the wider research into biochemical changes in the brain associated with depression are also highly revealing, indicating the brain's dynamic interaction with the environment. Using the Hamilton scale – a direct measure of the brain's biochemical state that indicates depression – in clinical trials drugs had a positive impact – but the same biochemical changes occurred in the brains of those in the control psychotherapy group: 'it is a nice example of the way in which talking can affect the body's biochemistry, just as changes in bio-chemistry can affect cognitive and affective processes.' This evidence shows that learning mechanisms such as talking directly impact on the biochemical mechanisms in the brain.

The evolution of learning

There may not be a sudden, revolutionary change in how people learn in the next few years, but there will be a revolutionary change in how learning is understood. The brain's integrated, dynamic interaction with its environment involves cognitive, emotional and health factors simultaneously. In learning, people are not acquiring facts but changing their brains and how they interact with their environments: learning is literally making minds.

How learning will change in the medium term is not clear. It will still be delivered by people, books, online materials, mass media and other methods, though the proportions of each are already changing – and will continue to do so. Many new learning experiences will be constructed differently: created by teams, global in approach and designed to appeal on many different levels, an approach already taken by many internet-based services such as BBC News Online. Big changes may come from unexpected applications of technology: digital learning environments that change dynamically in response to learner needs. Unfortunately access will remain a major issue for many people on earth: if you have no access to learning, you cannot learn; if you have poor learning skills, it will be difficult to learn; and in the medium term money will still be the dominant factor in access to learning experiences.

Yet with changes in delivery of learning, costs may fall as a percentage of gross domestic product for the services available, and that holds promise for those who are currently poor. The internet and other technologies will mean good learning experiences will be available everywhere (home, school and work), though people will have uneven experiences depending on the quality of human support they receive in any of these settings. It will be easier to give the learner control of their learning – its pace, the feedback and their pro-gress – though within defined limits. Dynamic changes in what and how people learn will occur frequently, based on new knowledge born of rigorous experimental or successful commercial approaches. The social and economic

Figure 9.2 For some the look and feel of learning is already changing

Source: courtesy of North News

environment in which learning occurs is rapidly changing; so are the means of accessing knowledge. There is also an acceleration of knowledge in science and technology, and learning should change rapidly, too.

In the economic world it is now a given that all economies can benefit from growth at the same time and that cooperation can bring success for all. The same principle is becoming accepted in many knowledge industries. More than ever, knowledge is global – internationally created, internationally used and internationally transmitted – and so it will be with learning. This does not mean that learning will become just simplistic universal generalizations. Knowledge is infinitely rich because, as Rose argues, 'There is more than one sort of knowledge, and we all need poetry art, music, the novel, to help us understand ourselves and those around us.'

There will always be challenges, too: learning will to some extent continue to evolve, and so it will never be possible to find an ultimate answer. The knowledge that learning must transmit will always be changing, and our needs as a society and individuals will be, too. Languages, cultures and the meanings they generate are constantly shifting, and so how learning is communicated will always remain something of an art. How people feel, their health and their wider environment all influence learning, and so learning needs to embrace art, fun, pleasure, wisdom, social learning, beauty and beautiful environments – all those things that are thought quintessentially human, and that are central to our sense of worth and self-belief. There are also issues of human rights: if learning becomes a much more powerful tool for shaping minds, it could be abused. A well-known example of this is the brain's capacity to register information subconsciously. Advertisers in the US used this capacity by creating subliminal messages. Although they were on screen for only about 14 milliseconds and people were not aware of seeing them, these messages did have an impact. Can we use such techniques in learning? It seems our initial response is 'no' (since we have a right to see – in this case literally – what we are learning). There will be other cases where powerful learning techniques may be put to unacceptable use (perhaps by cults and criminals). Legal questions might arise about the rights of children who might be forced to spend years learning useless things, and thereafter suffering economic disadvantage. Thus factors that have been largely ignored in the past – the damage done to a child's learning by parents, schools, economic deprivation, social exclusion and health, for example – may be issues that can no longer be ignored.

In the end, the benefits of mastering learning will be immense. The economic and social benefits for society are obvious, if only because of the improvement in human capital in a knowledge economy. Learning in childhood or in employment will be better, cheaper and faster than it is now, but also more flexible and engaging. The benefits for individuals will be equally important, from a personal sense of consistently making progress to mastering the learning itself. If learning experiences can influence attitudes and feelings, as surely they can, there is the prospect of improving the lives of people in the literal sense of helping them personally, socially, politically and emotionally – contributing to achieving their rights to 'life, liberty and the pursuit of happiness'.

Making minds

Understanding learning is mankind's greatest adventure because it will lead to understanding our minds, how they are made and their potential. The biological complexity of the human brain can now be understood using the knowledge and techniques created by the relentless advances in science, scientific technology and ICT. This is an evolutionarily important change, as it allows humans to adapt more effectively to their environment by mastering their learning. This ability to consciously make minds through understanding the unique nature of the brain will change our lives in fundamental ways, from the economic to the personal.

This understanding will come from the process of scientific investigation using the tools of social science and neuroscience, rather than from blind acceptance of conventional wisdom. This is a fundamental change in our world view, a scientific revolution that marks a shift in humanity's perception of itself. Understanding learning scientifically will mean clarity about how meaning is constructed by the brain, and the brain's development as a neuroscientific process. It will mean that people will be able to manipulate their learning and the learning of others.

However great the progress towards a perfect model for learning has been, people will not escape the human dilemma. The ethical issues of abuses of learning or attempts to own and commercialize aspects of learning will remain. The world will keep changing, too, with science, medicine and technology leading the way. Progress in learning will be the essential ingredient in the preservation of all our knowledge and achievements, and in efforts to improve all lives.

Advances in neuroscience and social sciences mean this is an era when the fundamental understanding of learning will change. To understand how minds are made and function is an extraordinarily arduous undertaking that will only be achieved through a cooperative international process – but it will be achieved. It will lead to better adaptation to the environment for individuals and for society. The quest to understand the human mind and how it works has been one of the central aspirations of humanity. What is now certain is that scientific processes powerful enough to establish this understanding exist, and are already beginning to reveal outcomes. It is a momentous time in human development for, as Ramachandran argued, this quest to understand ourselves is 'the greatest adventure that our species has ever embarked upon'.

Notes

Sources in general

These sources are designed to give starting points that will allow readers to explore some issues in greater depth. References are intentionally weighted to those available on the internet or to books in paperback. News is drawn from BBC News Online (http://news.bbc.co.uk) as the best free news resource, and newspapers cited are usually UK publications. Government or government agency publications are drawn from the relevant official websites, and associated research sites, such as the US Institute of Education Sciences (http://ies.ed.gov). University or other independent research, including articles from journals that are available free online, are drawn from the appropriate host site. The University of London's EPPI Centre reports, although not unique as good quality meta-analyses, are heavily used, and are all available online (http://eppi.ioe.ac.uk/cms). These are cited throughout as EPPI, name of first author (date), page number, rather than the very cumbersome formal citation recommended. Similar research evaluations are available online, such as the Cochrane Library, Institute of Education Sciences and elsewhere, though the range and quality varies, depending on the nature of the evaluations and the methods used. Monkseaton High School is an average state school in the north of England and is used to exemplify some issues rather than being held up as an exemplar of good practice. I have not provided detailed proofs of every argument in the book: I have confined myself to issues that I felt are more contentious.

Introduction

Specific reference is made to:

J. K. Galbraith, *The Affluent Society* (London: Penguin, 1998). Steven D. Levitt and Stephen J. Dubner, *Freakonomics* (London: Penguin, 2005): readers of this delightful book will immediately see the debt I owe to the first few chapters. I have taken the liberty of modifying Levitt's economic principles to fit education more exactly. I have also referred to it by its title rather than authors since it is more easily recognized. Vilayanur Ramachandran, *The Emerging Mind* (London: BBC, 2003), p. 26.

1 In the beginning: educational trial and error

Specific reference is made to:

Adaptedness: see Ernst Mayr, *What Evolution Is* (London: Orion, 2002). On genes, see BBC News, 9 September 2005: '"Proof" our brains are evolving'. The original research articles are: Patrick D. Evans *et al.*, '*Microcephalin*, a gene regulating brain size, continues to evolve adaptively in humans', *Science* 9, September 2005, pp. 1717–20; and N. Mekel-Bobrov *et al.*, 'Ongoing adaptive evolution of *ASPM*, a brain size determinant in *Homo Sapiens*', *Science* 9, September 2005, pp. 1720–2.

On theories of society 50 years ago: J. K. Galbraith, *The Affluent Society* (London: Penguin, 1998). On obesity: US Department of Health and Human Services, *The Surgeon General's Call to Action to Prevent and Decrease Overweight and Obesity* (Rockville, MD, 2001): US Department of Health and Human Services, Public Health Service, Office of the Surgeon General, www.surgeon general.gov/topics/obesity/calltoaction/CalltoAction.pdf; Statement of Lynn C. Swann, Chairman, President's Council on Physical Fitness and Sports, Office of Public Health and Science, US Department of Health and Human Services, before The House of Government Reform, 3 June 2004.

Intellectual potential: for the Flynn Effect – rising IQ scores: see Steven Johnson, *Everything Bad is Good for You* (London: Penguin, 2005); Flynn, J. R. (1999) 'Searching for justice', *American Psychologist* 54, pp. 5–20. David Riggs, *The World of Christopher Marlowe* (London: Faber, 2004); Peter Gay, *Mozart* (London: Orion, 1999).

Education, economic outcomes and social mobility: there is a very large literature on the subjects, but see, for England, Jo Blanden *et al.*, *Intergenerational Mobility in Europe and North America*, A Report Supported by the Sutton Trust, April 2005.

The economy's benefits: the knowledge/information society is a particularly popular analogy in the European Union, where it features in literally thousands of documents and research projects, but is also found worldwide as in OECD, *The Lifelong Learning Network* (Yokohama, 2002). For an introduction to Hikikomori, see BBC News Online, 20 October 2002.

Accelerating knowledge: Jon Kleinberg, 'Analyzing the scientific literature in its online context', *Nature*, www.nature.com/nature/focus/accessdebate/18.html.

For Moore's Law: ftp://download.intel.com/research/silicon/moorepaper.pdf. For dealing with extreme complexity using different modelling techniques, see Dana Mackenzie, 'Fight for the naked quark', *New Scientist*, 13 August 2005, pp. 32–5.

The Laura Spence story was reported so widely that it is impossible to list references. The question I am most frequently asked is how she is getting on. She was, and is, an exceptional person. Laura refused to be overwhelmed by the controversy – she wrote a column for a national newspaper, threw herself into her work and new sporting interests, and, once again, succeeded. I believe she was the first British woman to row for Harvard, and won a place in the 2003–4 Spring Academic All-Ivy Team. This meant she was one of only five women athletes chosen from Harvard (Academic All-Ivy's have 3.0 or better cumulative grade point average and have represented the university in regional or national sporting competitions). This achievement, in a different country, in a new sport and in a new education system, is a fitting tribute to someone who challenged prejudice in her home country and succeeded in the world's leading university. She currently studies medicine at Cambridge University. See www.oxfordstudent.com/tt2000wk3/news/imagine_if_they_did_it_to_you; *The Guardian*, 12 June 2000; T. R. Reid, *The Washington Post*, 1 June 2000; BBC News Online education reports for 26 May 2000; 3 July 2000; 4 August 2000; 25 November 2004 among others; *The Times*, 12 June 2004.

2 Education as segregation

Specific references are made to:

South Africa: www.services.gov.za/EducationAndTraining for South Africa's education system. The parallel with the US is interesting: see http://en. wikipedia.org/wiki/Brown_v._Board_of_Education for a brief overview, and judgement itself is clear: '[segregation of children in public schools] . . . deprive[s] children of the minority group of equal educational opportunities.' Many schools remain predominantly black or almost exclusively white because of the segregation that exists in communities, housing and society.

Measurement: see government education department web sites for claims about improvements.

Autism: *The Wall Street Journal,* 29 December 2003; *The Daily Telegraph,* 15 February 2004; and Graham Lawton, 'The autism myth', *New Scientist,* 13 August 2005, pp. 36–40. There are also a number of articles in the BBC News Online service on the MMR vaccine controversy that trace the origins and eventual rejection of one 'cause' of the epidemic. For the concept of 'tipping point', see Malcolm Gladwell, *The Tipping Point* (London: Abacus, 2003). See also *The Sunday Times*, 2 April 2006.

Subject ghettos: the quotation is from a Kenyan school's web site I felt it unfair to name. The Open University course on ICT T171 had over 10,000 students. S.-J. Blakemore and U. Frith, *The Implications of Recent Developments in Neuroscience for Research on Teaching and Learning*, Institute of Cognitive Neuroscience (London, 2000), p. 16 (hereafter Blakemore). This is a useful overview of research, though by no means the only study of its kind.

3 Globalizing learning

Du Fu: the translation is my own, though Dr Xiuping Li has advised me. Du Fu fits the Chinese image of the lotus in dirty water – someone who keeps their purity in a corrupt environment. Specific references are made to:

Steven Pinker, *The Language Instinct* (London: Penguin, 1995), p. 37, though Pinker's views on related issues are contentious. There are slight ('subtle' to quote the research) differences in neural pathways established for reading in different linguistic groups: see Blakemore, p. 40.

Learning from differences: Joseph Stiglitz, *Making Globalization Work* (London: Penguin, 2006) and later on Asian economic success; EPPI, Dyson (2002); OECD, PISA 2000 (web site given in text), but also see other OECD, EU and UN publications; Jeffrey Sachs, *The End of Poverty* (London: Penguin, 2005), pp. 18, 337.

Learning: see Blakemore (above); all quotations from the Open University use the course code, which makes them easier to find on the Open University web site (www.open.ac.uk) and are in the form the Open University course [code]: unit: page(s).

Learning is social: EPPI, Harlen *et al.* (2002), pp. 1–2 (a systematic review of the impact of summative assessment and tests on students' motivation for learning); emotional intelligence is, however, something very different from what is meant by emotion here: good explanations of emotion in learning are in OU SD 226, such as SD 226: Unit 6: 73 and Damasio, *Looking for Spinoza* (London: Random House, 2003), p. 54; ethical behaviours, pp. 160–5; see also Malcolm Gladwell, *Blink* (New York: Orion, 2005); Ernst Mayr, *What Evolution Is* (London; Penguin, 2002), p. 146; emotions imply something about the people we learn from. Some emotions have a clear social object, and it is interesting to see these in the context of education systems (see Table N.1).

One might think that in education none of the positive emotions is really allowed, and only the negative ones remain (contempt and – indirectly – disgust). Even where there are positive bonds in school, they are but a shadow of those in a family. School can be an emotionally disappointing environment.

ds. Quotations are from Liverpool's Medical Education web site and
ents, www.liv.ac.uk/facultymedicine.

rhaps useful to note that the pathways in the brain are not a single roll
. This is one of the reasons that the mathematics of cellular networks is
cult.

ates information is from UN figures.

re: See Karl Popper, *Conjectures and Refutations: The Growth of Scientific
dge* (London and New York: Routledge, 2002), pp. xi–xii, *passim*. In
ion, these 'severely critical tests' are, at the moment, those of social
e (not examinations). But how can we find the 'truth', if all we know are
istakes? Popper argued, as a philosopher might, that it all depends on
you think 'truth' is, but his answer was to adopt a mathematician's
tion, from Alfred Tarski: truth is that which corresponds most closely to
nown facts. This means, of course, that discovering our mistakes is a
ss that depends crucially on 'severely critical tests' that establish facts.

ucation as politics

al: see government web sites/state web sites for the positive spin stories,
ne research data bases for the real outcomes. A persistent, international
ng is that governments claim more success than is really justified (this is,
arse, true of schools as well).

re better?: UN Development Program, *Human Development Report 2003*,
: of a continuing series of reports.

ure: qualifications. EPPI, Harlen *et al.* (2002), p. 4, *passim*. The educa-
l web site of California (there are similar examples in most US states).

ure: The National Audit Office, *Making a Difference* (London, 2003) (www.
rg.uk/publications) and Ofsted web site (www.ofsted.org.uk). Similar
erns over social science-based research and other measures are evident in
JS:

Quality assurance in the conduct and evaluation of research. Peer review of
applications is the best guarantee of research quality. Peer review is taken
for granted in research in the physical and biological sciences and medicine.
It should be common practice in educational research as well . . .
Unfortunately, growing impatience in some quarters of the policymaking
community would prescribe research practice . . . Some members of Congress, for example, would mandate randomized trial experiments as the
gold standard of evidence. OERI and the Board urge policymakers not to
yield to this understandable impatience. They should be confident that

Table N.1 Emotions in the context of education systems

Emotion	Object	Respon
Attachment love	Caregiver	Keep c
Caregiving love	Offspring	Nurtur
Sexual love	Sexual partner	Engage
Disgust	Contamination	Reject
Contempt	Outgroup person	Treat w

Source: The Open University, SD 226: Unit 6: 73.

Building for learning: Sorrell Foundation (www.t
this is from a flyer); Mark Schneider, *Do School
Outcomes?* (NCEF, Washington DC, 2002), pp. 2,17
Designs see the DfES web sites (www.dfes.gov.uk) a

4 Education as prejudice

Grammar myth: see EPPI, Anderson *et al.* (2004), p
21st Century Brain (London, 2006), p. 134.

Why textbook answers are wrong: AAAS, Project 2
org/about/press and /publications/textbook/mgsci/re
Evaluations of Middle Grade Mathematics Textbooks.
February 2006.

Marks out of ten: EPPI, Harlen *et al.* (2002), pp. 4, 7.

Why children are violent: US Department of Health
Youth Violence: A Report of the Surgeon General, *passim*. C

5 Learning from mistakes

Joseph Stiglitz, *Making Globalization Work* (London: P

Learning from mistakes: National Educational Research
Board, *A Blueprint for Progress in American Education*
passim: Stiglitz, *op. cit.*, p. xvi.

Leadership: EPPI, Bell *et al.*, (2003) pp. 1–3, *passim*.

Effectiveness research: Daniel Muijs and David Reyno
(London: Paul Chapman, 2001), p. 57, *passim*.

Rich learning environment: www.whatworks.ed.gov has
have been subject to research, but most of the research d

rigorous standards, peer review, and methods appropriate to the subject being studied will produce research capable of generating powerful findings.

(*A Blueprint for Progress in American Education,* The National Educational Research Policy and Priorities Board, *US Department of Education,* Washington DC (2000), p. 7 cited in the text as NERPPB)

The impatience of politicians is, however, fully justified: after the hundreds of millions spent on educational research having apparently been almost entirely wasted, the desire to have clear outcomes is understandable. Nor is the research community's plea to be able to organize and control research without being accountable for its shortcomings adequate: learning is too important to wait for researchers to form a better system.

7 Free learning

Learning is a right: L. Campbell, D. Kyriakides, D. Muijs and W. Robinson, *Assessing Teacher Effectiveness* (London and New York: Routledge Falmer, 2004), p. 119.

The wind of change: Cambridge University Press: Richard Stone, *Some British Empiricists in the Social Sciences 1650–1900,* (Cambridge, Campbell *et al.,* 1997), p. 4.

Changing the world view: Thomas Kuhn, *The Structure of Scientific Revolutions* (3rd edn, Chicago: University of Chicago, 1996): Kuhn describes the process of advancement in sciences depending on changes of world view, or, as he describes it, a change of paradigm. As Kuhn points out about Science itself, revolutions in the fundamental paradigm, such as changing from an earth-centred view of the universe, or accepting Einstein's theory of relativity, have been long and hard processes of winning over a critical mass of scientists. It will be the same in learning: essentially, *Making Minds* argues that learning is undergoing a change of paradigm in Kuhn's terms. There are issues of detail as well: educational language and measurement lack international accepted standards, though an internationally understood descriptive language for education has been seen as necessary already. Globalized learning that is not culturally specific and related issues are discussed in many texts, for example: Nicholas Humphrey, *The Mind Made Flesh* (New York: Oxford, 2002), pp. 295–6, *passim*; for a scientist's argument, see Edward O. Wilson, *Consilience* (London and New York: Abacus, 1998) *passim*; for philosophers, see Andre Comte-Sponville, *The Little Book of Philosophy* (London: Heinemann, 2004), *passim* on ethics independent of religion and, on a less decisive but interesting level, Stephen Law, *The War for Children's Minds* (New York and Abingdon: Routledge, 2006), *passim* on the political and educational issues and *The Guardian* 25 April 2006.

New methods: it is relatively easy to present experiments in learning to parents and students as an additional learning experience when using a double-blind experimental method – one that is both rigorous and well researched because it is so frequently used in medical studies. Of course, new neurobiological technologies offer other approaches. *The Sunday Times*: 24 September 2006. For the Qwerty or path-dependence principle, see Paul Krugman, *Peddling Prosperity* (New York: W.W. Norton, 1995), p. 223.

Graceful exit: Daniel Muijs and David Reynolds, *Effective Teaching* (London; Paul Chapman, 2001), p. 222; for policy entrepreneurs see, for example, Krugman, pp. 10–15 and *Freakonomics*. With apologies to Juvenal, who was simply pointing out that the two did not go together in politicians.

8 The future of learning with technology

Technology and learning: the reference is for the British Museum's web site ref. ME 104096.

Panacea: Barrie Gunter and Jill McAleer, *Children and Television* (2nd edn, London and New York: Routledge, 1998) is one balanced account.

BBC and OU: see www.bbc.co.uk and www.open.ac.uk for further information on issues discussed in this chapter and others; K. Fairbank and M. Goldman, *China: A New History* (Cambridge, MA: Harvard University Press, 1998): for the cultural revolution 1966–76, pp. 383–405; for Keypoint schools, pp. 377–8: at both times the Chinese clung to an elitist educational model at the highest level, while espousing equality.

McEducate: as the BBC was created to give a technology content, so the internet was created to give newer technologies content and functions (that is to say, a Dell PC and Microsoft software benefit commercially by all the internet services the companies have not had to pay for or develop). Language learning using technologies seemed to have positive potential at Monkseaton High School, as its European Commission SAELN project (video conferencing, peer to peer) and Speak2Me project with Sitel (instructor to student) seemed to show: the basic principle was creating one-to-one conversations with a native speaker.

Adaptation to our IT environment: Intelligent Learning Environment (ILE); Professor Muijs is currently a Chair in Education at Manchester University; Carol Fitz-Gibbon, 'The need for randomized trials in social research', editorial for *Journal of the Royal Statistical Society* (Series A), 2004, 167, part 1, 4.

Readers of internet news may be more selective. It is likely that BBC News Online is more frequently accessed by younger people, and it may have a more international audience. It would be interesting to know if more news learning per minute takes place through this service in comparison to television or radio, as the comparison might indicate the strengths and weaknesses of the internet as a learning tool for general information. No doubt someone in the BBC knows the answers to these questions.

Experiment and conjecture is, of course, based on Karl Popper (and his use of Tarski's definition of truth): see citation above.

9 In the end

Opening: Steven Rose, *The 21st Century Brain* (London: Random House, 2006), pp. 151, 40, 154; an example of the issues in linking neurobiology and learning, in the same way that humans – like animals – have a tendency to focus on change in their environment, rather than things that are static or known; it may be that attracting and keeping the attention of learners isn't at all straightforward, nor simply a contrast between formal delivery of learning and delivery that mimics natural processes.

Maths: Blakemore, *passim*; Piaget, who misled most educationalists for many years since his experiments were crude and didn't look at behaviours in non-artificial situations, or even try to help the children learn (that is to say, if you can't do something at 8 doesn't mean you couldn't have learned it at 3). Try talking to a 4 year old about quarks – no problem; Eicholz *et al.*, *Element-ary School Mathematics* (Reading, MA: Addison-Wesley, 1968); Kelley *et al.*, *Elementary Mathematics for Teachers* (San Francisco, CA: Holden Day, 1970); and Continental Classroom, an NBC experiment in broadcast lectures in mathematics for students about to enter university was another interesting innovation at that time.

Finally, we began: Leo Standing's Power Function for memory may parallel the Power Law for Learning. R. Douglas Fields, 'Making memories stick', *Scientific American*, February 2005, pp. 58–63 (see also 'The other half of the brain', April, 2004) and the references cited in these articles; Steven Rose, p. 209; the heart presentation covered the names of major elements in the heart, the purpose and nature of the double circulation, and a comparison with single circulation in animals. There were seven questions on the post test, taken from an examination paper (see Table N.2). This does not prove anything, though it looks impressive (particularly in terms of the time it took). What it did do is convince me that this principle should be subject to a rigorous experiment. Russell Foster and L. Kreitzman, *Rhythms of Life* (London: Profile, 2005). *The Times Higher Educational Supplement*, 5 January 2007.

Learning as key: this section is speculation, of course, suggesting a clear shift from declarative to other forms of learning, and from facts to processes. The likelihood that information at our fingertips will make these more important

Table N.2 'Ten-minute break' research results, Monkseaton High School

Year 9 Experimental Group: *formative trial*	GCSE post test, using exam board marking scheme							
Questions correct	0	1	2	3	4	5	6	7
Percentage of trial class			4	13	8	38	29	8
Mark scheme GCSE C grade is 50%								
Academic potential measure suggests 60% of students should achieve at this level.	17% scored below 50%				83% scored above 50%			

Source: Monkseaton High School

than they have been underlies the argument. Arthur Conan Doyle, *The Complete Sherlock Holmes* (London, 2000), p. 21.

Drugs: Rose, pp. 254–63, 234, 164, 237 and *passim*; the Surgeon General's Report cited above, *passim*; I think Blakemore would forgive me for replacing 'teaching styles' with 'learning' here. In the previous chapter an intelligent learning environment based on existing digital technology was described. New functions have recently been added and aimed at analysing background factors and health, and their impact on learning. The health factors were measurements of electrical resistance – a very fast method recently developed and widely used by health professionals. This kind of approach creates a formidable research tool to identify how to improve learning, taking into account academic, emotional, health and external factors.

Finding our way: Rose, pp. 164, 237, 188; one of the outcomes of using an intelligent learning environment at Monkseaton High School was that it identified curriculum requirements that were inappropriate.

Final: Vilayanur Ramachandran, *The Emerging Mind*, (London: BBC, 2003), p. 26.

Acknowledgements

No book is the creation of a single human being, and no book begins at a single moment in time. I was taught to question by my family, had an interesting career in formal education on three continents, and have tried to help people learn from birth to 72 and from nursery through to university. I have learned from those experiences, and from the conversations and reading of a lifetime. I have been fortunate to have known many people who have had a passion for education – and for change – from different perspectives: researchers (David Reynolds, Barrie Gunter, Daniel Muijs); educational technology (Robin Moss); the DfES (Mukund Patel, Tim Dracup); and higher education (especially Liz Manning of the Open University). My colleagues and students have taught me more than anything else that education must change.

I am grateful for the help of people who have looked over drafts and commented: David Reynolds, Daniel Muijs, Jack Kenny, Laura Spence, Nancy Kelley, Toby Buckle, Kat Furness, Terry Whatson, Soraya Kazi, Sue Leaper and Philip Mudd. Two consultants helped in more detailed ways with *Making Minds*: Terry Whatson, the Open University, on the biology of learning; and Kat Furness, Monkseaton, on the images, tables and design. Philip Mudd at Routledge was a pleasure to work with, and had the vision to see that *Making Minds* could be a good book. Finally, my own family has contributed an enormous amount of time, patience and direct comment, and without Linda *Making Minds* would not have been written at all. All these people have reduced the number of errors and improved the quality of the book in many ways, and I am very grateful to them. On the other hand, the failures and omissions are mine.

Index

Page references in *italics* indicate illustrations.